3/4

THE HOME ART CROCHET BOOK

145 Old-Fashioned Designs
for Edgings, Insertions,
Borders, etc.

Edited by
FLORA KLICKMANN

Dover Publications, Inc.
New York

Copyright © 1990 by Dover Publications, Inc.
All rights reserved under Pan American and International Copyright Conventions.

Published in Canada by General Publishing Company, Ltd., 30 Lesmill Road, Don Mills, Toronto, Ontario.
Published in the United Kingdom by Constable and Company, Ltd., 10 Orange Street, London WC2H 7EG.

This Dover edition, first published in 1990, is a republication of *The Home Art Crochet Book: Containing Entirely New Designs for Lingerie, Edgings & Insertions, Borders for Tray Cloths & D'oileys, Deep Laces for Table Cloths & Valances, Motifs for Inlet Work and Irish Lace*, originally published by *The Girl's Own Paper & Woman's Magazine*, London, n.d. Several advertisements have been omitted and minor corrections have been made to several patterns. A new Publisher's Note has been written specially for this edition.

Manufactured in the United States of America
Dover Publications, Inc., 31 East 2nd Street, Mineola, N.Y. 11501

Library of Congress Cataloging-in-Publication Data

The Home art crochet book : 145 old-fashioned designs for
    edgings, insertions, borders, etc. / edited by Flora
    Klickmann.
        p.   cm.
    Originally published in the Girl's own paper & woman's
magazine.
    ISBN 0-486-26241-3
    1. Crocheting—Patterns.   I. Klickmann, Flora.
TT820.H7765   1990
746.43'4041—dc20   89-49084
                                                    CIP

Publisher's Note

Among the many women's magazines that flourished in the years just before World War I was *The Girl's Own Paper & Woman's Magazine*, published in London. In addition to the magazine itself, the same publishers also produced a number of books devoted to the "feminine" arts. One of these was *The Home Art Crochet Book*, which went through at least nine printings, attesting to the enormous popularity of crochet—a popularity that has in no way diminished.

Most of the patterns in the book are for edgings, insertions and borders, and are just as useful today as they were when they were originally published. The large selection of filet crochet motifs can also be easily adapted to modern uses.

The terminology used in the book is British and is not the same as the terminology used in the United States today. Generally, the names of the crochet stitches have "shifted" by one—the stitch known in the United States as "s c" is referred to as "d c" in the book, and "d c" is referred to as "tr." However, the original instructions were apparently written by different people and there is some variation in the terminology. For example, the terms "slip stitch," "single" and "s c" are all used to refer to the stitch we know in the United States as "slip stitch." A chart showing the modern American equivalents of the stitches can be found on page vii, along with a list of abbreviations used in the book and a crochet hook conversion chart.

Although, in most cases, the specific threads called for are no longer available, any of the designs can be made with regular crochet cotton. Linen threads used for lacemaking can also be used. Because no gauges are given, and usually no hook size is listed, it is sometimes impossible to determine what size thread was originally used for a particular pattern. However, since the designs do not have to "fit," this is not a major problem. Edgings can be made any size you wish, simply by varying the size of the thread and hook used—the finer the thread and the smaller the hook, the narrower the edging will be.

Section V, beginning on page 49, offers a number of designs combining crochet with various types of braid. Although such braids are not as popular as they were in the early part of the century, renewed interest in lacemaking has made many of them available once more. Any woven braid or ribbon can be used for the patterns on pages 49–52, while rickrack is a perfect substitute for the Vandyke braid called for on pages 53–61. Various picot, Honiton and other lace braids are available from distributors of lacemaking supplies. If you have difficulty locating them, they may be ordered by mail from Lacis, 2982 Adeline Street, Berkeley, CA 94703. The Rice braid and the Mignardise braid mentioned pose more of a problem, but you may be able to find a suitable replacement in a good notions or trimming store.

Before beginning any project, it is a good idea to make a small sample with the thread and hook that you plan to use. If your stitches are loose and untidy, use a smaller hook. If they appear crowded, use a larger hook. Keep making samples until you get the look you want.

Making a sample will also allow you to make sure that you understand the instructions (they do seem somewhat strange to modern eyes). If you have difficulties, study the photograph carefully. In most cases you can see the stitches clearly enough to understand how the piece was worked.

MARY CAROLYN WALDREP
Needlework Editor
Dover Publications, Inc.

ABBREVIATIONS USED IN BOOK

ch	chain
d or d c	double crochet
d tr	double treble crochet
long tr	long treble crochet
o	open mesh
quadruple tr	quadruple treble crochet
s	solid mesh
s c	single crochet
sp	space
tr	treble crochet
triple tr	triple treble crochet

STITCH CONVERSION CHART

Home Art's name	*Current American name*
chain	chain
single	
single crochet	} slip stitch
slip stitch	
double crochet	single crochet
treble crochet	double crochet
long treble crochet	
double treble crochet	} treble crochet
triple treble crochet	double treble crochet
quadruple treble crochet	triple treble crochet
miss	skip
catch into	slipstitch into

STEEL CROCHET HOOK
CONVERSION CHART

U.S. Size	British & Canadian Size	Metric Size (mm)
00	000	3.00
0	00	2.75
1	0	2.50
2	1	2.25
3		2.10
4	1½	2.00
5	2	1.90
6	2½	1.80
7		1.65
8	3	1.50
9		1.40
10	4	1.25
11		1.10
12	5	1.00
13		0.75
14	6	0.60

The Home Art Crochet Book.

Section I.

EDGINGS FOR THE AVERAGE WORKER.

Oyster-shell Edging.

1st Row.—15 ch, 1 d c into sixth ch from needle, 8 d c into next 8 ch, 5 ch, 1 d c into ch. Turn.

2nd Row.—5 ch, 1 d c into space of 5 ch, 9 ch, 1 d c into loop at end of row.

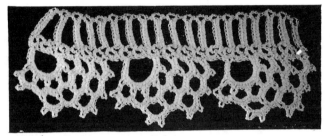

OYSTER-SHELL EDGING.

3rd Row.—5 ch, 9 d c into ch, 5 ch, 1 d c into loop.

Repeat from 2nd row for length required.

To form a Corner, if Needed.

Increase the space between bars by working * 5 ch, 1 d c into space, turn, 5 ch, 1 d c, turn, 5 ch, 1 d c, 9 ch, 1 d c into loop at end of row, 5 ch, 9 d c. 5 ch, 1 d c. Repeat from * twice. Then continue as before.

For Scallop.

Into the last two spaces at end of insertion work 3 d c, 18 ch, turn, 1 d c into first d c of those just worked : turn, work 5 loops of 5 ch separated by 3 d c into 18 ch, 3 d c into next space of insertion, turn, * 5 ch, 1 d c into loop of 5 ch. Repeat from * four times, 5 ch, turn, 3 d c, 5 ch, 3 d c, * 3 d c into next space. 5 ch, 3 d c. Repeat from * three times, 3 d c into space of insertion, turn, 5 ch, 1 d c into next 4 loops, turn, 5 ch, * 3 d c, 5 ch, 3 d c. Repeat from * twice, 3 d c into space of insertion, turn, 5 ch, * 3 d c, 5 ch, 3 d c. Repeat from * once, 3 d c into next two spaces. Repeat from beginning.

Rosette Edging. No. 202.

Use Ardern's No. 40 crochet cotton.

Start with 10 ch, making the first one very loose ; into it make 2 tr, 5 ch, 2 tr, 7 ch, 2 tr, 5 ch, 2 tr.

* Turn with 9 ch, and in middle sp make 2 tr, 5 ch, 2 tr, 7 ch, 2 tr, 5 ch, 2 tr. Repeat this row once.

ROSETTE EDGING.

Edgings for the Average Worker.

5 ch. into the side 9 ch make 6 loops of 16 ch, 8 ch, 1 d c into top of last loop, 3 ch, 5 tr into each loop, no ch between.

Turn at last tr, place 6 ch, 1 d c over each group of 5 tr below.

Turn and fill in with 7 d c in each sp. Catch the end of this row into adjoining scallop.

From the last d c, turn and make 8 ch, 1 d c over each group of d c below. Then fill in with 9 d c in each.

From the last d c ch 5, and go down to the middle sp ; into it make 2 tr, 5 ch, 2 tr, 7 ch, 2 tr, 5 ch, 2 tr. Repeat from *.

Add a straightening line at sewing-on edge of ch and d c.

Crochet Maltese Edging.

No. 40 crochet cotton. No. 6 crochet-hook.

Make 20 ch, turn the thread twice around the needle for a long tr, insert the hook through the fifteenth ch and pull the thread through ; then work off the loops on the needle, two at a time, retaining the last two loops on the needle ; form another long tr into the same ch stitch in the same way, then hook the thread through all the loops on the needle, * 5 ch, form 2 long tr through the first of these 5 ch in the same way as the last, 1 d c into the tenth ch of foundation, repeat from * twice and fasten to the tenth ch of the foundation, then repeat the loop

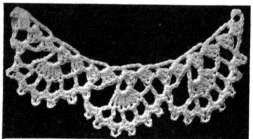

CROCHET MALTESE EDGING.

NARROW SCALLOPED EDGE. NO. 181.

into the first ch, * turn, make three of the groups of tr at each turning and fasten to the centre of the loop beneath with a d c, fasten a loop into each of preceding row and repeat from * four times.

After the last loop make only a group of tr, 10 ch, fasten with 1 d c to the end of preceding row, turn, and into this loop put 1 d c, 15 tr, 1 d c, then complete the row of loops to the top, turn and work a row of loops into last row and around the semicircle of tr, putting a loop into the 3rd, 7th, 11th and 15th tr, fasten a group to the end of the loop to the left, turn, * 8 ch, 1 d c into centre of first loop on the semicircle, 8 ch, fasten these to the beginning of the first 8 ch, and over this loop of double ch work 1 d c, 15 tr, 1 d c. Repeat from * three times.

This completes the pattern which is repeated from the first row. Finish with a row of 1 tr into each loop at the top, followed by 6 ch, then over the ch stitches work a row of 10 d c into each space.

Narrow Scalloped Edge. No. 181.

Use Ardern's No. 36 crochet cotton.

Make 7 ch, into the first make 3 tr, 3 ch, 1 tr.

Turn with 5 ch, make 7 tr in first space, * 3 ch, 3 tr, 3 ch, 1 tr into next space.

Turn with 6 ch, make 3 tr in first

2

sp, 3 ch, 1 tr in top of 3rd tr below, 3 ch, 1 tr into 1st of the 7 tr below, 3 ch, 1 tr into 3rd tr below, 3 ch, 1 tr into 5th tr, 3 ch, 1 tr into 7th tr, 3 ch, catch into lowest picot loop on previous scallop. In the case of the first scallop, end with 1 tr into last space, as there is no previous scallop to catch over to.

Turn with 1 ch, fill in each of the 7 space below with 2 d c, 4 ch, 2 d c, then make 3 ch, and put 3 tr, 3 ch, 1 tr into last sp.

Turn with 6 ch. make 3 tr, 5 ch, 1 tr into first sp.

Turn with 5 ch, make 7 tr in first sp, and repeat from *.

Coronet Baby Edging.

Chain 18 and join in a ring. Ch 9, treble twice into the 9th chain of the ring. (This will give three straight lines of equal length.) Make one double crochet between the two trebles. (This will form a tiny ring into which the following loops are to be made.) Make 4 loops of 18 ch each, fastening each with a double crochet into the tiny ring. Ch 9, and then make 3 double crochet into the top of the 4th loop. (This again will give three straight lines of equal length.) Ch 9, and then make 3 double croc-het into the top of next loop, repeat-ing this for each of the loops. Into each of the 9 ch made between the loops, make three double crochet, ch 6,

3 double crochet, ch 6, 3 double crochet. (The double crochet are all placed close together, so that the in-tervening 6 chain in each case has the appearance of a picot above the edge).

This completes the 1st scallop, which differs slightly from the re-maining scallops. The second scallop (and the remaining scallops) are made as follows : * Ch 18 and join into a ring. Ch 9 ; treble twice into 9th ch of the ring. Make one double crochet between the two trebles. Make 4 loops of 18 chain each, fastening each with a double crochet into the tiny ring. Ch 9, and then make 3 double crochet into top of 4th loop ; ch 9, and make 3 double crochet into each of the next *two* loops. Make one double crochet into the first picot (*i.e.*, the 6 chain between the sets of 3 double crochet) of the previous scallop. Into each of the 9 chain between the loops make 3 double crochet, ch 6, 3 double crochet, ch 6, 3 double crochet. Repeat from *.

Mimosa Edging.

Ch 7 and join in a ring, * ch 7, 4 treble into the ring, ch 3, 1 treble into ring, ch 3, 1 tr into ring.

2nd Row.—Ch 7, 4 trs into the second space, ch 3, 1 tr also into second space. ch 3, 1 tr into the first

CORONET BABY EDGING.

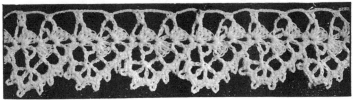

MIMOSA EDGING.

of the 4 tr in previous row. Ch 3, 1 tr into the last of the 4 tr in previous row, *ch 3, 1 tr into the loop at the end of previous row, repeat from * 3 times (making 4 times in all).

3rd Row.—* 2 d c, ch 5, 2 d c, into the first space formed by the 3 ch in the

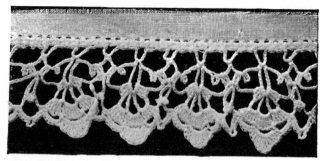

A LACY EDGE. NO. 214.

previous row. (The d c to come close together for the intervening 5 ch to form a picot.) Repeat from * into each of the remaining six small spaces. The last little picot loop (*i.e.*, the 5 chain between the double crochets) forms the ring for the commencement of the next scallop. This ends the first scallop; for the remaining scallops go back to the beginning, and repeat from * to the end of the 2nd row. Then make 1 d c into the 6th picot of the previous scallop (this is to unite the scallops), then proceed with directions for 3rd row as already given.

To Form the Edge for Sewing on.

When the work is the required length, make 7 ch and alternately 2 trs and 2 d c into each of the loops at the lower edge of the pattern; the double to go into the long loops and the trebles into the alternate short loops.

A Lacy Edge.

Use Manlove's No. 36 lace thread.

This is worked upon a foundation chain the length required, or into hem-stitching, or featherstitch braid.

1st Row.—Make a d c into foundation, then ch 12 to form a loop, * d c, ch 2, d c, ch 2, d c, ch 12. Repeat from *.

2nd Row.—Into 1st loop of 12 ch, make a loop of 16 ch, * then ch 12, catch back into 5th to form a picot, ch 7, catch into next loop of 12 ch, ch 12, catch back into 5th, ch 7, catch into next loop of 12 ch, and into this same loop make a loop of 16 ch. Repeat from *.

3rd Row.—* Into top of long loop make 3 tr, 5 ch, 1 long tr (thread twice over needle), 5 ch, 1 long tr, 5 ch, 2 ordinary tr. Then ch 7, make 2 tr on the inner side of picot, and 2 more tr beside next picot, ch 7 and catch into next long loop. Repeat from *.

4th Row.—* In the 1st 5 ch make 5 tr, in the next put 7 tr, and into the next 5 tr. Then ch 12, catch back into 5th for picot, ch 7, catch between the two sets of tr in row below, ch 12, picot, ch 7. Repeat from *.

5th Row.—Over each 5 tr make 5 ch, with 7 ch over the 7 tr; 2 d c in the ch nearest the tr on each side, and 7 ch between them.

6th Row.—Fill the 5 ch with 5 d c, into the 7 ch made 3 ordinary tr, 4 long tr, 3 ordinary tr. Fill in the intervening 7 ch 4 d c, 5 ch, 4 d c.

Deep Scallop Edging for Tablecloths.

Use D.M C thread No. 12. and with a medium fine crochet-hook

Make 27 ch, turn, 1 tr into the nineteenth ch, 2 ch, 1 tr into each third ch.

Turn, 5 ch, 1 tr into next tr, 2 ch, 1 tr into next tr, 2 tr into next 2 ch, 1 tr into next tr, 2 ch, 1 tr into next tr, 2 tr into next 2 ch, 1 tr into next tr, 2 ch, 10 tr into next space.

Turn, 4 ch, 1 tr into next tr, 1 ch, 1 tr into each of next 9 tr, 2 ch, 1 tr into next tr, 2 ch, 1 tr into third tr, 2 ch, 1 tr into next tr, 2 ch, 1 tr into third tr, 2 ch, 1 tr into next tr and next third ch.

5 ch to turn, 1 tr into next tr, 2 ch, 1 tr into next tr and each of next 2 ch and next tr, 2 ch, 1 tr into next tr, each of 2 ch and next tr, 2 ch, 1 tr into each 1 ch space to the top.

5 ch to turn, 1 tr into next space, 2 ch, 1 tr into each of next eight spaces, 2 ch, 1 tr into next tr and into each third stitch to the end.

5 ch to turn, 1 tr into next tr, 2 ch, 1 tr into next tr, 1 tr into each of 2 ch and next tr, 2 ch, 1 tr into next tr, 1 tr into each of next three stitches, 2 ch, 1 tr into next tr, 2 ch, 1 tr into next tr, 1 tr into each stitch to the top.

Turn, 5 ch, 1 tr into third tr, 2 ch, 1 tr into every third tr to the end of the consecutive tr, 2 ch, 1 tr into each third stitch to the end.

5 ch to turn, 1 tr into next tr, 2 ch, 1 tr into next tr, next 2 ch and following tr, 2 ch, 1 tr into next tr, next 2 ch and following tr, 2 ch, 1 tr into next tr, 3 ch, 1 d c into next tr, 3 d c into each space to the top.

6 ch to turn, 1 long tr into third d c, 2 ch, 1 long tr into every second d c,

DEEP SCALLOP EDGING FOR TABLECLOTHS.

2 ch, 1 tr into next tr, 2 ch, 1 tr into each third stitch to the end.

5 ch to turn, 1 tr into next tr, 2 ch, 1 tr into next tr, next 2 ch and next tr, 2 ch, 1 tr into next tr, 2 ch and next tr, 2 ch, 1 tr into next tr, 2 ch, 1 tr into next tr, 3 tr into each space to the top, 10 tr into last space.

Turn, 6 ch, into next sixth tr and every sixth tr following put 2 tr, 2 ch, 2 tr, with 3 ch between the groups of tr, 3 ch, 1 tr into last of the consecutive tr, and 2 ch, 1 tr into every third stitch to the end.

5 ch to turn, 1 tr into next tr, 2 ch, 1 tr into next tr, and into the 2 ch and following tr, 2 ch, 1 tr into next tr, 2 ch and following tr, 2 ch, 1 tr into next tr, 2 ch, 1 tr into next tr, 3 ch, and repeat last row from this to the top, putting the groups of tr into the space between the 2 tr.

Turn, 9 ch, picot 6 of them, 1 tr into space between the tr, 6 ch picot followed by a tr, twice into same space, * 3 ch, 1 d c over centre of the two chains beneath, 3 ch, 1 tr followed by a 6 ch picot into next space three times, then 1 tr into same space, and repeat from *.

Work three rows of the seven meshes at the upper portion, and then repeat from the first row, taking in the ends of the picots in the preceding scallop to the end of the last row of tr.

Lace for Underclothing.

Very suitable for trimming nightgowns, ladies' and children's knickers, bedroom napery, etc., is this design worked with No. 12 D.M.C. cotton perle. Use a medium fine crochethook, and make 27 ch.

Turn, 1 tr into the twenty-fourth

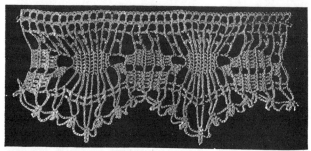

LACE FOR UNDERCLOTHING.

ch, 5 tr into next 5, 2 ch, miss 2, 6 tr into next 6, 7 ch, miss 7, 1 tr into next, 2 ch, miss 2, 1 tr into next.

Turn, 5 ch, 1 tr over last tr, 3 ch, 1 tr into the fourth ch, 3 ch, 1 tr into next 6 tr, 2 ch, 6 tr into next 6, 10 ch, turn, 1 tr into next tr, miss next tr, 4 tr into next 4, 2 ch, 4 tr into next 4, 7 ch, 1 tr into last tr, and 2 ch, 1 tr into next third ch.

5 ch to turn, 1 tr over last tr, 3 ch, 1 tr into next fourth ch, 3 ch, 1 tr into the ch before the tr, 4 ch, 1 tr into the last of the 4 tr each of the 2 ch and next tr, 4 ch, 1 tr into next tr, 1 ch, 1 tr into next ch.

10 ch, turn, 1 tr into next tr, 2 ch, 1 tr into next tr, 7 ch, 5 d c over next 5 ch, 7 ch, 1 tr into last tr, 1 ch, 1 tr into next third ch.

5 ch, turn, 1 tr into next tr, 3 ch, 1 tr into fourth ch, 3 ch, 2 d c into next d c, 3 d c into next 3, 2 d c into next

d c, 7 ch, 1 tr into next tr, 2 ch, 1 tr into next tr.

10 ch, turn, 1 tr into next tr, 2 ch, 1 tr into next tr, 7 ch, 1 d c into each of next d c, 7 ch, 1 tr into last tr, 2 ch, 1 tr into third ch.

5 ch, turn, 1 tr into next tr, 3 ch, 1 tr into fourth ch, 3 ch, 1 d c into each d c, 7 ch, 1 tr into next tr, 2 ch, 1 tr into next tr.

15 ch, turn, 1 tr into next tr, 2 ch, 1 tr into next tr, 7 ch, 7 d c into next 7, 7 ch, 1 tr into last tr, 2 ch, 1 tr into third ch.

5 ch to turn, 1 tr into next tr, 3 ch, 1 tr into third ch, 3 ch, 7 d c into the d c, 7 ch, 1 tr in next tr, 2 ch, 1 tr into next tr.

12 ch, turn, 1 tr. into next tr, 2 ch, 1 tr into next tr, 7 ch, 1 d c into each of next d c, 7 ch. 1 tr into last tr, 2 ch, 1 tr into third ch.

5 ch, turn, 1 tr into next tr, 3 ch, 1 tr into fourth ch, 3 ch, 1 d c into each d c, 7 ch, 1 tr into next tr, 2 ch, 1 tr into next tr.

7 ch, turn, 1 tr into next tr, 2 ch, 1 tr into next tr, 7 ch, miss first d c, 1 d c into each of next 5 d c, 7 ch, 1 tr into last tr, 2 ch, 1 tr into third ch.

5 ch, turn, 1 tr into last tr, 3 ch, 1 tr into fourth ch, 3 ch, 1 tr into next d c, 3 ch, 4 tr into next 4 ch, 2 ch, 1 tr into next tr, 2 ch, 1 tr into next tr.

7 ch, turn, 1 tr into next tr, 1 tr into next tr and each of 2 ch and following tr, 2 ch, 1 tr into next third tr and into each of the 3 following ch, 7 ch, 1 tr into last 2 tr, 2 ch, 1 tr into next third ch.

5 ch, turn, 1 tr into next tr, 3 ch, 1 tr into fourth ch, 3 ch, 1 tr into second and third ch and 4 tr, 2 ch, 1 tr into each of next four tr and 2 tr into the last tr, 3 ch, turn, 1 tr. into second and following 4 tr, 2 ch, 6 tr into next 6, 7 ch, 1 tr into last tr, 2 ch, 1 tr into third ch.

5 ch, turn and repeat from the second row.

For the edging, join the thread to one of the loops and make 6 ch, fastening with 2 d c to next loop, and repeat along this end, putting the 6 ch into each loop and into the 3 ch in the centre of the group of tr, work a second

A NOVEL EDGING.

row or chain loops over the first, putting 10 ch in each and fastening to the d c of last row with a 7 ch picot into the second d c.

For the heading 3 d c into each space at the top, then a row of 1 ch, 1 tr into every second tr, finishing with 2 d c into each space.

A Novel Edging. No. 204.

This edging can be worked in Ardern's crochet cotton No. 36.

1st Row.— 16 ch, 4 tr into 7th ch from needle. Make 3 spaces by working 3 ch, miss 2 ch, 1 tr into next 3 times.

2nd Row.—6 ch, 1 tr on 1st tr, 2 spaces (3 ch, miss 3 ch. 1 tr on tr), 3 ch, 4 tr, 3 ch, 1 tr into last sp.

3rd Row.—6 ch, 4 tr into 1st sp, 5 sp.

4th, 5th and 6th Rows are worked in same way, increasing 1 sp every row.

7th Row.–Work the same as last rows, but in the 6th space of last row 4 tr, 2 more sp.

8th Row.—6 ch, 4 tr into 2nd sp, 3 ch, miss 4 tr, 4 tr into next sp, 5 sp, 3 ch, 4 tr 3 ch 1 tr into last sp.

9th Row.—6 ch, 4 tr into 1st sp, 7 sp, 3 ch, miss 4 tr, 4 tr into sp, 2 sp.

10th Row.—6 ch, 1 tr on 1st tr, 10 sp, 3 ch, 4 tr 3 ch 1 tr into last space.

11th Row. — 6 ch, 1 tr on 1st tr, and work 3 sp only for next point. Repeat from 2nd row.

When required length is obtained work a square on either side of points as follows : * 1 tr on 5th tr from point, 1 sp 3 ch 4 tr into next sp, 2 sp.

2nd Row.—6 ch, 4 tr in 2nd sp, 3 ch, miss next sp, 4 tr in next, 1 sp.

3rd Row.—Same as 1st row.

4th Row.—5 sp.

Work same 4 rows on other side of point, working from point. Repeat from * to end of points. Into every sp work 3 d c except corner sp, when work 6 d c.

For square between the two points formed by squares just worked—

1st Row.—1 d c into middle d c of corner sp (see illustration), 15 ch, 1 d c into corresponding sp of next square.

2nd Row.—5 sp along ch.

3rd Row.—1 sp, 3 ch, 4 tr into 3rd sp, 2 sp.

4th Row.—6 ch, 4 tr into 2nd sp, 3 ch, miss 1 sp, 4 tr into next sp, 1 sp.

5th Row.—2 sp, 4 tr, 2 sp.

6th Row.—5 sp.

7

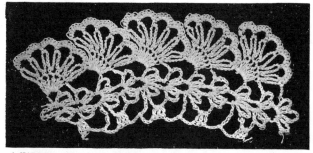

A NARROW SCALLOPED EDGE.

Work 3 d c into each sp except corner sp, into which work 6 d c.

Repeat to end of work.

For Fancy Edge.

1st Row.—1 d c into 1st corner sp of square worked on side of 1st point, 8 ch, 1 d c into 2nd d c of middle sp, 16 ch, 1 d c into same d c, 8 ch, 1 d c into next corner sp, 8 ch, 1 d c into 2ud d c of middle sp, 16 ch, 1 d c into same d c, 8 ch, a loop of 16 ch into corner sp, 8 ch, loop of 16 ch into middle sp, 8 ch, loop of 16 ch into corner sp, 8 ch, loop of 16 ch into middle sp, 8 ch, 1 d c where squares join, 8 ch, loop of 16 ch into middle sp, 8 ch, join the two points of squares with 1 d c. Repeat from beginning of row.

2nd Row.—Into 1st loop of 16 ch work 3 tr, * 4 ch, 3 tr, 4 ch, 3 tr 4 ch 3 tr 4 ch 3 tr into next loop. Repeat

from * 4 times, 4 ch, 3 tr into next loop, 3 tr into next. Repeat from * to end of work.

3rd Row.—1 d c into 1st 4 ch, 7 tr into 4 ch between the 3 tr, 7 ch into next 4 ch, 7 ch into next 4 ch, 1 d c into next 4 ch. Repeat from beginning of row. Work 6 d c on the 6 tr between squares.

A Narrow Scalloped Edge.

Ch 12, join in a ring, 6 ch, 1 tr into the ring, 4 ch, 2 tr, 6 ch, 2 tr, 4 ch, 1 tr.

2nd Row.—6 ch into the second ch of the 1st row, 1 tr, 4 ch, 2 tr, 6 ch, 2 tr, 4 ch, 1 tr, 4 ch, and into the first 6 ch of the 1st row 6 tr.

3rd Row.—* 12 ch, 1 d c into the last tr of 2nd row, * 12 ch, 1 d c into next tr of 3rd row. Repeat from * until there are six loops. 6 ch, 1 d c into sixth ch at last loop, connect the loops with 5 ch between and 1 d c into sixth ch of each loop.

4th Row.—Over each bar of 5 ch of the last row 6 d c, 4 ch into the middle 6 ch of the 2nd row, 1 tr, 4 ch, 2 tr, 6 ch, 2 tr, 4 ch, 1 tr.

5th Row.—6 ch into the 6 ch of the 4th row, 1 tr, 4 ch, 2 tr, 6 ch, 2 tr, 4 ch, 1 tr, 4 ch, and into the 4 ch of the 4th row, made after the row of double crochet over the short bars of 5 ch, 6 d c, and repeat from *. For the edge * 3 tr into the first loop of 6 ch, 4 ch, 1 long tr, 4 ch, 3 tr,

Repeat from *.

A NARROW LACE EDGE.

A Narrow Lacy Edge.

1st Row.—6 ch, join in a ring, 6 ch, 3 tr into the ring just made, 4 ch, 3 tr into the same ring.

2nd Row.—* 6 ch, 5 d c into the 4 ch of the 1st row, 4 ch, 1 tr into the 6 ch of the first row, 4 ch. 1 tr into the same 6 ch.

3rd Row.—6 ch, 3 tr into the last 4 ch of the 2nd row, 4 ch, 3 tr into second 4 ch of the previous row. Repeat from * for the length required.

One edge of the work is straight, and the opposite edge has loops of 6 ch along its length.

4th Row.—Into the first of these loops 1 d c, * 12 ch, 1 d c, 12 ch, 1 d c, then 10 ch, 1 d c into the fourth ch of this row of 10 ch, 5 ch and 1 d c into the next loop. Repeat from *.

5th Row.—1 d c into the first loop of the 4th row, * 5 ch, 1 d c into the next loop, 9 ch, 1 d c into next long loop. Repeat from *.

6th Row.—Over each 5 ch of the 5th row do 5 d c, over each 9 ch of the 5th row, 3 d c, 5 ch, 3 d c, 7 ch, 3 d c, 5 ch, 3 d c. Place the double crochet stitches close together so that the 5 ch and 9 ch form little rings.

A Simple Narrow Edging.

For this design use No. 40 crochet cotton and a No. 6 hook. Form 6 ch into a ring, 6 ch, 3 triple tr into the ring (thread three times over the needle), work off two loops at a time, retaining the last on the needle until the third is formed, finally drawing the thread through the four loops on the needle, 7 ch, 4 triple tr into the ring, five times more, 7 ch, 1 d c over first trs, 5 ch, 1 tr into next ch, 5 ch,

1 tr into fourth ch, 5 ch, 1 tr into same ch, 5 ch, 1 tr over next trs, 2 ch, 1 tr into same stitch as last, 5 ch, 1 tr into fourth ch, 5 ch, 1 tr over next trs, 5 ch, 1 tr into same stitch as last, 5 ch, 1 tr into next fourth ch, 5 ch, 1 tr into ch before the trs, 2 ch, 1 tr into the trs, 5 ch, 1 tr into the fourth ch, 5 ch, 1 tr into same ch, 5 ch, 1 tr into next trs, 2 ch, 1 tr into next ch, 5 ch, 1 tr into fourth ch, 5 ch, 1 tr into next trs, 5 ch, 1 tr into same trs, 5 ch, 1 tr into

A SIMPLE NARROW EDGING.

fourth ch, 5 ch, 1 d c into third ch of the first five, 5 d c over 5 ch, and 3 d c over each 2 ch all round, with a 5 ch picot in the centre of the 5 ch spaces where there are 2 tr into the same stitch.

Each motif is joined to the preceding in the centre of a picot.

To fill in the spaces at top, working from left to right, join the thread to the first picot, 20 ch, form last eight into a ring, turn, * 6 ch, 1 triple tr through the first of the ch, 1 d c through loops on needle, 1 d c over second tr on motif, 6 ch, 1 triple tr through first ch, 1 d c through top, 3 d c into the ring, * repeat into the second next tr on this motif and into corresponding tr on side of next motif, 1 d c into the ring, 12 ch, 1 d c

Edgings for the Average Worker.

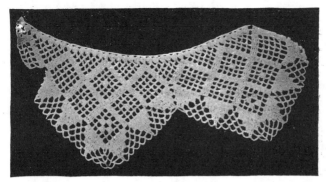

PLAID LACE.

into picot on next motif, then repeat to the end.

Work a row of d c closely over the chain stitches, then make the straightening row of 2 ch, 1 tr into every third d c. Finish with a row of 2 d c into each space.

Plaid Lace.

Foundation of 29 ch.

1st Row.—4 tr into seventh ch from needle, 3 ch, miss 3 ch, 19 tr into next 19 ch.

2nd Row.—6 ch, 1 tr into fourth tr, make sp of 3 ch, miss 2 tr, 1 tr into next tr, work 3 more sp in the same way, 3 tr on next 3 tr, 3 ch, 1 tr on tr, 3 ch, 4 tr, 3 ch, 1 tr into loop of 6 ch.

3rd Row.—6 ch, 4 tr into first 3 ch, 3 sp, 3 tr on 3 tr, 5 sp.

4th Row.—6 ch, 1 tr on tr, 4 sp, 3 tr on 3 tr, 3 sp, 3 ch, 4 tr, 3 ch, 1 tr into loop of 6 ch.

5th Row.—6 ch, 4 tr, 5 sp, 3 tr on tr, 5 sp.

6th Row.—6 ch, 1 tr, 4 sp, 3 tr on tr, 5 sp, 3 ch, 4 tr, 3 ch, 1 tr into loop.

7th Row.—6 ch, 4 tr, 3 ch, miss 3 tr, 1 tr into fourth tr,* 2 tr into sp, 1 tr in tr. Repeat from * to end of row.

8th Row.—6 ch, 1 tr, 4 sp, 3 tr on

3 tr, 5 sp, 3 tr, 1 sp, 3 ch, 4 tr, 3 ch, 1 tr.

9th Row.—6 ch, 4 tr. 3 sp, 3 tr, 5 sp, 3 tr, 5 sp.

10th Row.—6 ch, 1 tr, 1 sp, 3 tr in sp, 2 sp, 3 tr, 2 sp, 3 tr in sp, 2 sp, 3 tr, 3 sp, 3 ch, 4 tr, 3 ch, 1 tr.

11th Row.—6 ch, 4 tr, 5 sp, 3 tr, 5 sp, 3 tr, 5 sp.

12th Row.—6 ch, 1 tr, 4 sp, 3 tr, 5 sp, 3 tr, 5 sp, 3 ch, 4 tr, 3 ch, 1 tr.

13th Row.—6 ch, 4 tr, 3 ch, miss 3 tr, 1 tr in next tr, * 2 tr in sp, 1 tr on tr. Repeat from * to end of row.

14th Row.—6 ch, 1 tr, 4 sp, 3 tr, 5 sp, 3 tr, 5 sp, 3 tr, 1 sp, 3 ch, 4 tr, 3 ch, 1 tr.

15th Row.—6 ch, 4 tr, 3 sp, 3 tr, 5 sp, 3 tr, 5 sp, 3 tr, 2 sp, 3 tr into sp, 2 sp.

16th Row.—6 ch, 4 tr into second sp, 1 sp, 3 tr into sp, 1 sp, 3 tr on tr, 2 sp, 3 tr into sp, 2 sp, 3 tr, 5 sp, 3 tr, 3 sp, 3 ch. 4 tr, 3 ch, 1 tr.

17th Row.—6 ch, 4 tr, 5 sp, 3 tr, 5 sp, 3 tr, 5 sp, 3 tr, 2 sp, 3 tr into sp, 2 sp.

18th Row.—6 ch, 1 tr, 4 sp, 3 tr, 5 sp, 3 tr, 5 sp, 3 tr, 5 sp, 3 ch, 4 tr, 3 ch, 1 tr.

19th Row.—6 ch, 4 tr, 3 ch, miss 3 tr, 1 tr on fourth tr, * 2 tr into sp, 1 tr on tr. Repeat from * 5 times.

Repeat from 2nd row for length required.

Edging Round Point.

1st Row.—1 tr on fourth tr of strip of 4 tr, * 2 tr into space, 1 tr on tr, Repeat four times, 6 ch, miss 3 tr, 1 tr on fourth, 15 tr into spaces as before,

10

6 ch, miss 3 tr, 1 tr into fourth, 12 tr. This brings you to space at bottom of point. Into this space work 3 tr, 6 ch, 3 tr, 13 tr, 6 ch, miss tr, 16 tr into spaces, 6 ch, miss tr, 16 tr as before, 16 tr into next spaces, and continue row to end of length.

2nd Row.—1 tr on third tr of last row, 11 tr on next 11 tr, * 6 ch, 1 d c into 6 ch, 6 ch, miss 2 tr, 1 tr on next tr, 11 tr. Repeat from * to end of row, but do not work any chain between points.

3rd, *4th*, and *5th Rows.*—The same as 2nd row, but work 8 tr, and 3 loops of 6 ch, 4 tr, and 4 loops of 6 ch, 2 tr, and 5 loops of 6 ch, respectively.

Dotted Lace.

Use Ardern's No. 30 Cotton.

Make chain rather longer than length required.

1st Row.—1 d c into twenty-fourth ch from needle. * 18 ch, miss 5 ch, 1 d c into next. Repeat from * to end of row.

2nd Row.—24 ch, 4 tr into loop of 18 ch, * 18 ch, 4 tr into next loop. Repeat from * to end of row.

3rd and *4th Rows.*—Same as 2nd row.

5th Row.—Same as 2nd row, but begin with 7 ch instead of 24 ch.

6th Row.—8 ch, 1 d c into loop of 18 ch, 3 loops of 18 ch into same loop, * 18 ch, 3 loops of 18 ch into next loop. Repeat from * to end.

7th Row.—8 ch, * 4 tr into first loop, 5 ch, 4 tr into next loop, 1 d c into 18 ch. Repeat from * to end.

8th Row.—3 ch, 1 d c into 5 ch, 18 ch, 1 d c into next 5 ch, 10 ch, catch into 5th ch from needle to form picot, 5 ch, 1 d c into next 5 ch.

Repeat the 6th, 7th, and 8th rows once.

Fine Lace Border suitable for Underwear.

The heading is worked in Manlove's No. 60 cotton, the remainder in No. 100.

Heading.

Chain 8, join in a ring by making into first chain 1 tr, 3 ch, 1 tr.

* Turn with 7 ch, make 4 d c into first space, 3 ch, 4 d c into second space.

Turn with 6 ch into first space, make 4 d c, 3 ch, into next space 1 tr, 3 ch, 1 tr. Repeat from * till heading is required length.

Scallops.

Into the first little loop made by the 6 ch on the lower edge of the heading * make a loop of 18 ch. Then ch 10, catch back to fourth chain and form a picot. Ch 5, catch into next loop of six chain at bottom of heading and repeat from * all along the length of the heading.

Into each fourth loop * make 7 loops of 18 ch each, on completing the seventh loop ch 5, carry across the back and catch into base of first loop, ch 9, carry up side of first loop, make 5 tr into top of each loop.

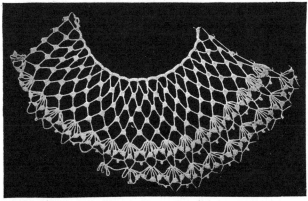

DOTTED LACE.

Edgings for the Average Worker.

Turn after completing last 5 tr, ch 6, carry it across 5 tr of previous row and catch into space between. Work round scallop in this way, on reaching the other side of scallop, catch into the next loop of 18 ch suspended from the heading.

Turn, fill in each 6 ch with 3 d c, 5 ch, 3 d c, 5 ch, 3 d c. Fasten to next loop of 18 ch [on opposite side suspended from the heading].

Ch 10, catch back into fourth loop for picot, ch 5, catch into next loop suspended from heading, ch 10, catch

A FINE LACE BORDER FOR UNDERWEAR.

back into fourth loop, ch 5, catch into next loop of 18 ch suspended from heading. Repeat from *.

A Good All-Round Edging.

Use Ardern's No. 24 Cotton.

Insertion.

13 ch, 1 d c into sixth from needle, 6 d c into ch, 5 ch, 1 d c into ch. Turn.

2nd Row.—5 ch, 1 d c into first space, 7 ch, 1 d c into space at end of row.

3rd Row.—5 ch, 7 d c into ch, 5 ch, 1 d c into space. Repeat 2nd and 3rd row for length required.

The Scallop.

Work on side of insertion with only one row of spaces, 4 d c into four spaces of insertion, 1 d c into next space, 18 ch, 1 s c into first d c just worked, 3 d c, 5 ch, 18 d c into 18 ch, 1 d c into same space as before, 16 ch, 1 s c into 3 d c from loop of 5 ch in previous bar, 3 d c, 5 ch, 16 d c, 1 d c into same space, * 14 ch, 1 s c into third d c as before, 3 d c, 5 ch, 4 d c into 14 ch, 1 d c into space. Repeat from * twice, 4 d c into next five spaces of insertion, and repeat from beginning, leaving one space of 4 d c between each set of bars.

An Effective Tray-cloth Edging.

Use Manlove's No. 42 Cotton.

Ch 9, join in a ring, turn with 7 ch, and into the ring make 4 tr, 4 ch, 1 tr, 4 ch, 1 tr.

* Turn with 7 ch, and into first space make 4 tr, 4 ch, 1 tr, 4 ch, 1 tr. Then make 4 ch, and into the end outside space make 12 tr, turn with 14 ch, and into top of each of 12 tr of previous row make a loop of 14 ch, making 12 loops in all.

After making the 12th loop ch 4, and into the next space make 4 tr, 4 ch, 1 tr, 4 ch, 1 tr.

Turn with 7 ch, into first space make 4 tr, 4 ch, 1 tr, 4 ch, 1 tr, then ch 7, 1 d c into top of first loop, 1 d c into second loop, ch 7, 1 d c into third loop, 1 d c into 4th loop, ch 7, 1 d c into fifth loop, 1 d c into sixth loop, ch 7, 1 d c into seventh loop, ch 7, 1 d c into eighth loop, ch 7, 1 d c into ninth loop, 1 d c into tenth loop, ch 7, 1 d c into eleventh loop. 1 d c into twelfth.

Turn and fill in each of the 7 chain

A GOOD ALL-ROUND EDGING.

in the top of each tr, 3 tr in the 3 ch, then in next sp make 3 tr, 3 ch, 1 tr, 3 ch, 1 tr.

of previous row with 4 d c, 2 loops of 14 ch each, and 4 more d c. On reaching the last 7 ch in previous row, fill this with 7 doubles. In next little space make 4 tr, 4 ch, 1 tr, 4 ch, 1 tr.

Turn with 7 ch, and into first space make 4 tr, 4 ch, 1 tr, 4 ch, 1 tr, ch 9, and catch with a d c into first long loop in previous row, ch 9, 1 d c into second loop, 1 d c into third loop, ch 9, 1 d c into fourth loop, 1 d c into fifth loop, ch 9, 1 d c into sixth loop, 1 d c into seventh loop, ch 9, 1 d c into eighth loop, 1 d c into ninth loop, ch 9, 1 d c into tenth loop.

Turn, fill each 9 ch in previous row with 3 d c, 5 ch, 3 d c, 5 ch, 3 d c, 5 ch, 3 d c. Fill in five spaces in this way, and fill in last 9 ch with 9 d c. Into next little space make 4 tr, 4 ch, 1 tr, 4 ch, 1 tr. Repeat from *.

Shell Edging.

Use Ardern's No. 36 cotton, and No. 5 hook.

1st Row.—Start with 7 ch, making the first one loose; into this make 3 tr, 3 ch, 1 tr, 3 ch, 1 tr.

2nd Row.—Turn with 6 ch, into first sp make 3 tr, 3 ch, 1 tr, 3 ch, 1 tr. 3 ch, and in last sp make 8 tr.

3rd Row.—Turn with 3 ch, make 2 tr

4th Row.—Turn with 6 ch, into first sp make 3 tr, 3 ch, 1 tr, 3 ch, 1 tr. 3 ch, 1 tr into top of the 3rd tr below, then 1 tr into top of every other one below, putting 2 ch between each.

5th Row.—Turn with 3 ch, in each sp put 3 tr right along to the central loop in outer edge, in which is put the usual 3 ch, 1 tr, 3 ch, 1 tr.

6th Row.—Same as 4th Row.

7th Row.—Turn, put 2 d c into each sp, with 4 ch between, end with the usual 3 tr, 3 ch, 1 tr, 3 ch, 1 tr into last sp.

8th Row.—Turn with 6 ch, into 1st sp make 3 tr, 3 ch, 1 tr, 3 ch, 1 tr.

Repeat from 2nd Row.

Add a straightening line at sewing-on edge of ch and 2 tr in each loop.

Simple Linen Crochet Lace.

This design is worked on a length of chain stitches with fine linen crochet thread and a hook to correspond

AN EFFECTIVE TRAY-CLOTH EDGING.

13

SHELL EDGING.

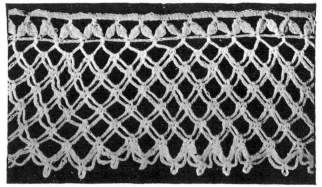

SIMPLE LINEN CROCHET LACE.

Make a d c at the end of the chain, * 5 ch, insert the hook through the first of the 5 ch and form a long tr, repeat the tr through the same ch, and draw the thread through all the loops on the needle, 5 ch, repeat the 2 long tr through the first ch, fasten this loop to next fifth ch on the foundation, and repeat from *.

2nd Row.—1 d c into centre of first loop, * 4 ch, 1 d c into next loop. Repeat from *.

3rd Row.—10 ch, 1 d c, into each d c of last row.

4th Row.—10 ch, 3 d c into each loop of last row.

5th Row.—1 d c into the centre of the 3 d c, * 5 ch, 1 d c into the top of the loop, 5 ch, 1 d c into the centre of the 3 d c. Repeat from *.

6th Row.—* 1 d c before, into and after the d c on the top of the loop, 10 ch. Repeat from *.

7th, 9th, 11th and 13th Rows are the same as the 5th. 8th, 10th and 12th Rows are the same as the 6th.

14th Row is the same as the 12th, but is worked over with a row of 10 d c into each loop, and 3 ch between the loops.

In the last row, fasten the thread to the centre d c between the loops with 1 d c, * 7 ch, 1 d c into the top of the loop between the fifth and sixth d c, 7 ch, 1 d c into same place, 7 ch, 1 d c into centre d c between the loops. Repeat from *.

Section II.

UNCOMMON INSERTIONS.

A Narrow Waved Insertion.

For this insertion, suitable for trimming underclothing, use No. 70 linen crochet thread and a fine hook. Make a ch of the required length.

A NARROW WAVED INSERTION.

1st Row.—2 ch 1 tr into every third ch.

2nd Row.—* 1 d c into first space, 5 ch, 1 long tr into second next sp, 5 ch, 1 long tr into same sp, 5 ch, 1 d c into second next sp, * and repeat to the end.

3rd Row.—* 1 tr into the next fourth and fifth ch, next long tr and next 3 ch (6 tr in all), 5 ch, 1 tr into same ch as last, and 1 tr into each of next five stitches, miss last 3 ch of this loop and first three of next, then repeat from *.

4th Row.—* Miss first tr, 1 tr into each of next five, 5 ch. 1 tr into each of next 5 tr, miss next tr, and repeat from * to the end.

5th Row.—8 ch, * 1 long tr into next third tr, 5 ch, 1 d c into the 5 ch loop, 5 ch, 1 long tr into next third tr, and repeat from *.

6th Row.—2 ch 1 tr into every third stitch.

Then finish

both sides with a row of 3 d c into each space.

A Narrow Block Insertion.

Use Ardern's No. 36 crochet cotton.

This simple but very useful insertion consists entirely of solid and open spaces. Start by making 4 open sp of 1 tr, 2 ch each, upon a foundation ch.

2nd and *3rd Rows.*—1 open sp, 7 tr, 1 open sp. Turn at the end of each row with 6 ch.

4th Row.—4 open sp. Repeat from 2nd row.

Fill in the edges with 3 d c in each sp.

Leaf and Bar Insertion.[1]

Begin with a chain of 63 stitches.

1st Row.—Ch 2, d c once into the 2nd[2] and then into 3rd ch. Then * ch 2, skip 2 ch, and in the next ch make 1 d c. Repeat from * seven times, making 8 holes; d c six times along the row. Make 4 holes (*i.e.*, ch 2, skip 2 ch, make 1 d c in the next ch); d c 6 times along the row, 3 holes, 1 d c into each of the 2 remaining ch.

Always start the line with 2 ch, 1 d c into the 2nd d c, 1 d c

A NARROW BLOCK INSERTION.

---

[1] In this pattern, the term "d c" refers to the same stitch known as "d c" in modern American terminology.

[2] This will be the 4th ch from the hook.

Uncommon Insertions.

into the 3rd d c of previous line.

Finish each line with 1 d c into each of the 3 last d c of previous line.

2nd Row.—3 holes, 12 d c along the row, 4 holes, 3 d c, 7 holes, finish the line as above.

3rd Row.—7 holes, 6 d c, 2 holes, 3 d c, 2 holes, 6 d c, 3 holes.

4th Row.—3 holes, 3 d c, 3 holes, 6 d c, 1 hole, 6 d c, 7 holes.

5th Row.—7 holes, 6 d c, 1 hole, 6 d c, 3 holes, 3 d c, 3 holes.

6th Row.—3 holes, 3 d c, 3 holes, 6 d c, 1 hole, 6 d c, 7 holes.

7th Row.—5 holes, 3 d c, 1 hole, 6 d c, 1 hole, 6 d c, 2 holes, 3 d c, 4 holes.

8th Row.—4 holes, 3 d c, 2 holes, 6 d c, 1 hole, 6 d c, 1 hole, 3 d c, 5 holes.

9th Row.—4 holes, 3 d c, 2 holes, 6 d c, 1 hole, 6 d c, 1 hole, 3 d c, 5 holes.

10th Row.—5 holes, 3 d c, 1 hole, 6 d c, 1 hole, 6 d c, 2 holes, 3 d c, 4 holes.

11th Row.—3 holes, 3 d c, 3 holes 6 d c, 1 hole, 6 d c, 7 holes.

12th Row.—7 holes, 6 d c, 1 hole, 6 d c, 3 holes, 3 d c, 3 holes.

13th Row.—3 holes, 3 d c, 3 holes, 6 d c, 1 hole, 6 d c, 7 holes.

14th Row—7 holes, 6 d c, 1 hole, 3 d c, 3 holes, 6 d c, 3 holes.

15th Row.—4 holes, 12 d c, 3 holes, 3 d c, 7 holes.

16th Row.—8 holes, 18 d c, 5 holes.

17th Row.—4 holes, 3 d c, 1 hole, 18 d c, 7 holes.

18th Row.—9 holes, 6 d c, 1 hole, 3 d c, 1 hole, 6 d c, 3 holes.

19th Row.—3 holes, 9 d c, 1 hole, 21 d c, 5 holes.

20th Row.—4 holes, 18 d c. 2 holes, 3 d c, 1 hole, 6 d c, 3 holes.

21st Row.—4 holes, 3 d c, 1 hole, 9 d c, 2 holes, 6 d c, 6 holes.

22nd Row.—4 holes, 9 d c, 1 hole, 3 d c, 1 hole, 15 d c, 4 holes.

23rd Row.—5 holes, 3 d c, 1 hole, 15 d c, 1 hole, 9 d c, 3 holes.

24th Row.—4 holes, 3 d c, 1 hole, 18 d c, 7 holes.

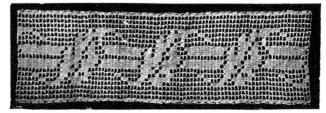

LEAF AND BAR INSERTION.

Repeat from the beginning of the first row.

Cog-Wheel Insertion.

Chain 7, join in a ring, turn with 5 ch, and into the ring make 8 tr, 5 ch, 1 tr.

* Turn with 7 ch into the space in previous row, make 2 tr, 5 ch, 4 tr, ch 2. Into the top of each of the 8 tr in previous row make 1 tr with 2 ch between each. Then 4 tr in the next space.

Turn with 5 ch, make 2 doubles into each space made by 2 ch in previous row, ch 5, carry this across 4 tr in previous row, and in next space make 8 tr, 5 ch, 1 tr. Repeat from *.

Care must be taken in joining, as the pattern meets exactly.

Waved Festoon Insertion.

For a Tea-cloth this could be worked in No. 36 cotton and No. 5 hook. Worked in a fine cotton, or linen

COG-WHEEL INSERTION.

loops of 18 ch with
5 loops of 6 ch.

The Fans.

Into each loop of
18 ch work 1 d c in
order to draw the 5
loops together.
From the fifth d c
work 6 ch, and
catch into the first
d c. Into this ring work 9 tr; then
ch 4, and into the top of each of
the 9 trebles work 1 tr with 1 ch between each; and counting the 4 ch
you turned with as 1 tr, this gives
you 9 spaces to work into. Turn
again, and into each space in previous
row put 2 tr.

Turn with 5 ch, and put 1 tr into
each space in previous row, with 2
ch between each tr.

Fasten at the end on to the waved
centre stripe, and then go back with
a row of 4 ch and 2 d c into every
space. There should be 18 spaces
in all.

The Sewing-on Edge.

* Leave 4 spaces at the outside of
the fan. Start in the 5th space and
work to the 14th space, putting 2 tr
into each space, with 1 ch between.
Then ch 7, and join to the edge of

thread, or silk, this is very pretty as
a dress trimming.

The waved stripe running through
the centre is worked first. After this,
the fans are worked in place, one at
a time, the thread being broken off
on the completion of each fan and
the end worked in neatly. The edge
for sewing on is added last of all.

The Waved Stripe.

Ch 6 and join in a ring.

Turn with 6 ch, and into the ring
work 2 tr, 3 ch, 2 tr, 3 ch, 2 tr, 3 ch,
2 tr.

* Turn with 18 ch, and into first
space work 2 tr, 3 ch, 2 tr, 3 ch, 2 tr,
3 ch, 2 tr.

Turn with 6 ch, and into first space
work 2 tr, 3 ch, 2 tr, 3 ch, 2 tr, 3
ch, 2 tr. Repeat from * four times
(making five times in all), which will
give you 5 loops of 18 ch.

Continue the pat-
tern in this way,
only now turn with
6 ch on the side
you worked the 18
ch before; and turn
with 18 ch on the
side you worked the
6 ch before. Do this
five times, and re-
verse again. In this
way work as long
a strip as you re-
quire, alternating 5

WAVY FESTOON INSERTION.

17

Uncommon Insertions.

the waved stripe (you can see where by studying from the illustration) with 2 tr ; then 7 ch and join to next loop in waved stripe with 2 doubles, then 7 ch, and join to next loop with 2 tr. Then ch 7 and proceed to the next fan by repeating from *.

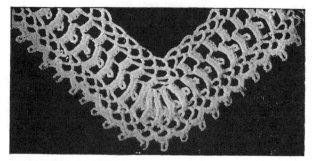

NARROW BAR INSERTION.

Finally, fill in all the way along the sewing-line with doubles.

Narrow Bar Insertion.

This is suitable for letting into linen, or as a foundation for other patterns.

Ch 26 and form a ring, and into this ring work the following :—Ch 7, 1 d c, ch 6, 5 d c, ch 6 (this forms a picot between the two sets of 5 d c), 5 d c, ch 6, 1 d c, ch 6, 1 d c.

2nd Row.—Ch 6, 1 d c into first little space ; ch 6, 5 d c into second space ; ch 7, 1 d c into third space ; ch 6, 1 d c into fourth space.

3rd Row.—Ch 6, 1 d c into first space ; ch 6, 5 d c into second space ; ch 6, 5 d c likewise into second space (the doubles are all placed close together, so that the intervening 6 chain has the appearance of a picot) ; ch 6, 1 d c into third space ; ch 6, 1 d c into end space.

When the work is the required length the outside edge is finished as follows :—3 d c, ch 6, and 3 d c in each little space.

If a corner is wanted, it is made by turning the work on completing the long bar only ; this is done three times. When the 7 ch is next made, continue beyond it as before, so as to make the space for the short bar, as at first starting.

A Graceful Insertion.

1st Row.—9 ch, join in a ring. * 18 ch, 1 d c into ring. * Repeat 5 more times. 9 ch, 1 d c into ninth ch of the last 18 ch, * 5 ch, 1 d c into 9 ch of second loop of 18 ch previously made. Repeat from * until the 6 loops are connected.

Into the 5 ch of 2nd line, * 3 d c. 6 ch, 3 d c (the 6 ch to form a small loop). Repeat into each 5 ch, connecting the long loops.

4th Row.—18 ch into the second small loop of 3rd row, 1 d c, * 18 ch, 1 d c, 18 ch, 1 d c, 18 ch, 1 d c, 18 ch, 1 d c into the fourth loop. Repeat from *, 9 ch, 1 d c into 9 ch of last 18 ch, 1 d c into second and third loops, 8 ch, 1 d c into the ninth ch of connecting line of 18 ch of previous row, 18 ch, 1 d c into fourth loop, 1 d c into fifth loop, 1 d c into sixth loop, 6 ch, 1 d c into each d c of previous line over the 3 loops, 4 d c over connecting chain of previous line, 10 ch, 1 d c back into fourth ch of this line, 5 ch, 4 d c over connecting chain of previous line, 1 d c over each of the previous d c above the loops.

18 ch, make 1 d c into central loop formed by catching back into the 4 ch of line of 10 ch of previous row.

For the sewing-on edge do a row of chain, and into each long loop of 18

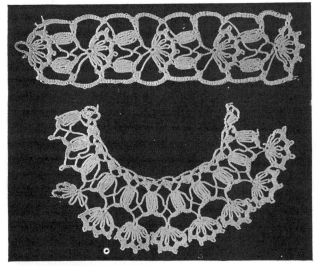

A GRACEFUL INSERTION WITH
EDGING TO MATCH.

ch do 3 tr into the outer small loops;
between the lines of 18 ch do 2 trebles.

Cover this row of chain with double
crochet.

Edging to Match
the Insertion.

Foundation.—7 ch and join in a
ring, 7 ch, 3 tr into the ring, 6 ch,
* 1 tr into the second 7 ch previously
made, 3 ch, 1 tr into the same space,
7 ch, 3 tr into 3 ch previously made,
6 ch, repeat from * until the required
length is made.

1st Row.—Into each of the 6 ch of
the foundation 1 d c, * 18 ch, 1 d c,
18 ch, 1 d c, 18 ch, 1 d c into next 6 ch
of the foundation. Repeat from *.

2nd Row.—* 1 d c over ninth ch of
each long loop of 18 ch, 9 ch, 1 d c
over ninth ch of connecting line of
18 ch, 9 ch, 1 d c into the next group
of 3 loops. Repeat from *.

3rd Row.—* 3 d c into the 3 d c of
previous row, 4 d c over the first 4 ch
of the line of 9 ch. 10 ch, catch back
into the 5th ch of this line of 10 to
form a small ring, 5 ch, 4 d c over last

**For all kinds
of Lingerie.**

4 of 2nd row of 9 ch
of last line. Repeat
from *.

4th Row.—Into each
of the small rings make
5 loops of 12 ch each,
catching each loop into
the ring with 1 d c.
Between each set of
loops do a line of 10 ch.

5th Row.—1 d c into
first loop, 5 ch, 1 d c
nto next loop, 5 ch.
Continue till the line
is completed.

6th Row.—3 d c into
* 5 ch of previous line,
5 ch (these form a little
ring), 3 d c into the same 5 ch. Fill
each 5 ch of the 5th line in this way.
After repeating this 3 more times do
1 d c into the 5 ch of the connecting
line of 10 ch of the 4th row. Then
3 d c into the first of the next group
of 5 ch between the long loops.
Repeat from *.

Shamrock Insertion
and Lace.

Use medium fine crochet thread for
this insertion and lace, which is very
suitable for trimming underclothing,
nightgowns, and children's garments.
Make * 10 ch, form 7 into a picot, 12
ch, form 7 into a loop, into which put
three loops of 7 ch each, fasten each
with 1 d, and put the last d immediately before the first of the first
loop, cross over to the right side and
put into each of the three loops 1 d,
15 tr, 1 d, 12 ch, form 7 into a picot,
1 ch, fasten after the picot before the
trefoil with 1 d, 10 ch, picot 7, 10 ch,
picot 7, and repeat from *. Join the
first leaflet on each trefoil to the last
on the preceding in the eighth stitch,
by putting the hook through the

19

Uncommon Insertions.

eighth stitch on the latter, and pulling the thread through. When the first row is of the required length, commence the second at the other side in the same way, and join the " filling " between the two centre picots at the corresponding part in the second row of " filling."

For the edge 1 tr into the fourth tr, on the centre leaflet of the first trefoil, 6 ch, * 1 tr into the fourth tr from the other side of same leaflet, 6 ch and repeat from * at both sides. Then into each 6 ch space work 8 d. Next row, 1 tr into first d, 2 ch, 1 tr into every third d. Finish with 3 d into each space.

The corresponding lace edging is worked the same as the first row of the insertion. For the second row make a tr between the first two picots, 3 ch, 1 tr at each side of every picot and stem.

4 d into each 3 ch space.

1 tr into first d, 2 ch, 1 tr into every third d.

3 d into every 2 ch space.

For the lower edge fasten the thread to the fourth last tr on the first leaflet, * 10 ch, 1 d into centre of top leaflet, 10 ch, 1 d into next fourth tr on next leaflet, 5 ch, 1 d into fourth tr on next leaflet, and repeat from * to the end. Commencing at the first of the last row, 7 d, 6 ch, * 10 d into next loop, 6 d into next, 8 ch, turn these back to the right and fasten to the sixth d from end of preceding loop, turn, and into this top loop work 6 d, 6 ch, 6 d; then into the loop beneath continue working 4 d, 6 ch, 7 d.

Into next loop, 5 d, 6 ch, 5 d, and repeat from *.

SHAMROCK INSERTION AND LACE.

FOR ADVANCED WORKERS.

THE BELL-FLOWER DESIGN.

Bell-Flower Design.

For this design use Strutt's No. 36 Belper Super Crochet Cotton.

Commence with the Narrow Bar Insertion described on page 18.

When the insertion is the required length, work a Large Cone and a Turkey Tail, as follows, starting the cone in the tenth space along the heading.

The Large Cone.

1st Row.—Ch 8 and join in a ring; into this ring make 16 loops of 18 ch each. Then ch 9, and catch into the top of last loop made, * ch 6 and catch into next loop, and repeat from * till all the loops are united at the top with 6 ch between.

2nd Row.—Ch 6 and catch into centre of the 6 ch in previous row. Ch 6 and catch into next space made by 6 ch in previous row; then make 5 d c with 6 ch between into the next 9 spaces, finishing the row with 6 ch into each of the two remaining spaces.

(Note that each row is to be a space less than the previous row, so as to narrow the design and bring it to a cone-shaped point.)

3rd Row.—Ch 6 and catch into the 2nd space made by the 6 ch in the previous row. Repeat this throughout the row.

4th Row.—Ch 6 and catch into space in previous row, ch 6 and catch into next space; then make **5 d c** with 6 ch between into the next 7 spaces, and end with 6 ch into 2 remaining spaces.

5th Row.—Like 3rd Row.

6th Row.—Like 4th Row, but make the d c into 5 spaces only.

In this way narrow the cone off until there are only 3 plain holes.

Now work down the left side of the cone, filling in the little straight spaces with 3 d c only, and the jutting out spaces with 3 d c, 6 ch and 3 d c (the 6 ch to form what looks like a picot between the 2 sets of 3 d c). In the same manner work up the other side of the cone till the point is reached.

The Turkey Tail.

From the apex of the cone the Turkey Tail is formed as follows :—

1st Row.—Start as for the large cone by making 16 loops of 18 ch each.

2nd, 3rd, and *4th Rows.*—Consist of net work only, *i.e.*, 6 ch caught into each space in previous row, but no d c.

5th Row.—Make a loop of 18 ch, then 5 d c into the first space in the previous row. Repeat the loop and 5 d c into each space throughout the row.

6th Row.—Ch 9 and catch into top of last loop; then * ch 7, and catch into next loop. Repeat from * throughout the row.

7th Row.—Make 4 d c, 7 ch, 4 d c, and 7 ch into each space in previous row.

Count ten spaces along again, and into the tenth make a loop of 16 ch, and into this work two small cones, following the directions given for the first cone, but making only 9 loops for each at the start, instead of 18.

The Bell Flower also depends from this centre loop of 16 chain.

To form the Bell.

Make two loops of 22 ch each into the central ring to form the stem on which the bell hangs. Join these two loops at the bottom with 6 ch. This forms the start for a Turkey Tail, which, when joined (with a needle and cotton), forms the round bell.

The 5 stamens inside the bell are lengths of chain worked in coarser cotton and fastened off with a knot at the end. These should be long enough to show below the edge of the bell.

An Edging for a Toilet Cover.

This design consists of rings of roses filled in with picot stitch and joined together in any length. Picot stitch filling is again used on one side of the edging according to the width of lace desired, then finished off with a border of roses which forms the edge to be sewn on the toilet cover.

Ardern's No. 24 crochet cotton is used, and a crochet hook No. 4.

The Central Rose.

Form 6 ch into a ring.

1st Row.—Work 6 ch, 1 tr in the ring, then 3 ch, 1 tr, making 6 divisions and finishing with 3 ch, a slipstitch in the 3rd of 6 ch.

2nd Row.—Work 1 d c, 4 tr, 1 d c in each division.

3rd Row.—Work 5 ch, 1 d c at the back and between each division.

4th Row.—Work 1 d c, 8 tr, 1 d c for each petal.

5th Row.—Work 10 ch, * a slipstitch in the 5th from the needle, 2 ch, 1 d c in the middle of a petal, 7 ch, a slipstitch in the fifth from the needle, 2 ch, 1 tr between 2 petals, 7 ch. Repeat from * and finish with a slipstitch in the 3rd of 10 ch.

6th Row. Work 11 ch, * a slip-stitch in the 5th from the needle, 3 ch, 1 tr on d c, 8 ch, a slip-stitch in the 5th, 3 ch, 1 tr on tr; 8 ch. Repeat from * and finish with a slip-

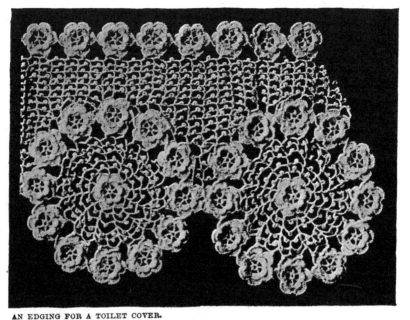

AN EDGING FOR A TOILET COVER.

stitch in the 3rd of 11 ch.

7th Row.—Work 10 ch, * a slip-stitch in the 5th, 7 ch, a slipstitch in the 5th, 2 ch, 1 tr on tr, 7 ch. Repeat from * and finish as in last row.

8th Row.—Work 11 ch, * a picot in 5th, 3 ch, 1 tr between 2 picots, 8 ch, a picot in 5th, 3 ch, 1 tr on tr, 8 ch. Repeat from *.

9th Row.—Work 11 ch, * a picot in 5th, 3 ch, 1 tr on tr, 8 ch. Repeat from * and break off.

Now work a rose as first described, and in the last row join the middle of a petal to one picot of the central design; also join the next petal to the next picot. Make another rose and join it in a similar manner to the next two picots of the central design and to one petal of the previous rose.

Complete the ring according to the illustration.

Make another ring and join it to two petals of one rose, and continue to make a length of lace as desired.

The Filling-In.

Begin where two roses join, making tr, picot and ch backwards and forwards in order to keep the work flat and even and in a line with the top rose of the rings. Then work about 6 rows of picot stitch, 7 ch, a picot in the 5th, 2 ch, 1 tr.

Work and join a line of roses according to the illustration, and the design is complete.

Fan Edging.

The specimen piece was worked in No. 80 sewing cotton.

1st Row.—Ch 12 and join in a ring; into this make 7 loops of 12 ch each. * Stroke these loops so that they lie quite regular and even.

2nd Row.—Ch 6 to lead up, and catch with a d c into the top of last loop made. Then * ch 5 and catch with a d c into top of next loop. Repeat from * till all the loops are united.

For Advanced Workers.

3rd Row.—Make another row of holes by making 5 ch and catching with a d c into spaces made by the chain in previous row. Make 7 spaces in all by catching the final d c into the top part of the "lead-up" chain.

4th Row.—Make 6 d c in each of the spaces in previous row.

5th Row.—Ch 7, 1 d c in between each tiny semicircle in previous row; complete row in this way.

6th Row.—8 d c into each 6 of the spaces made by the 7 chain in previous row. Into the remaining space make 7 loops of 12 chain each and repeat from * in the 1st row above. This starts the next fan.

By making these 7 loops into that last little space each fan is formed so that it falls naturally into its right place. Five of these fans are formed on each side—*i. e.*, ten in all—to form the pattern. But much depends on the size of the cotton used : if a much coarser cotton is used, then the depth of the lace need only be eight or even six fans in all. The worker will soon see what depth of lace is best suited to the purpose she has in view.

For the next row of fans, commence in exactly the same way, only the second and each alternate

fan is joined to the corresponding one in the previously completed row. This is done when you are working the outer edge of the fan. At the second little scallop draw the loop of cotton on the needle through the corresponding scallop on the completed row, and again join them when making the third scallop. In this way each row is united as you work down them to the lower edge of the lace. Study the illustration, and you will see which way the fans face when joined, and how it produces a pretty effect of tabs at the lower edge.

To make an even line at the top of the lace, for sewing it on to material, * make 12 ch from the corner of the fan to its central ring ; then 20 chain to dip down and carry it to the corner of next lower fan ; then 7 ch, to unite it across with corner of second fan in next row ; 20 ch more to carry up to central ring of top fan in second

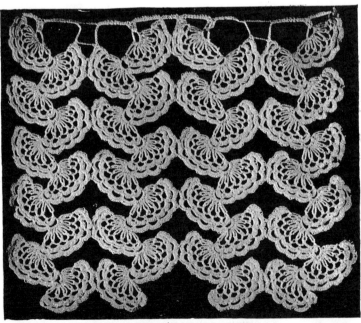

FAN EDGING : SUITABLE FOR FIVE O'CLOCK TEA-CLOTHS AND OTHER HOUSEHOLD LINEN.

row; 12 ch to carry it on to corner of
this fan; 7 ch to join to top corner
of top fan in third row and repeat
from * the whole length of the edging.

Then return, working d c over
all the chain made; but when you
come to the dips, do not make
d c right down into these, but
chain 7 across to form the square and
proceed with d c into the upper
part of the 20 ch below. The object
is to form a straight edge at the very
top, with no dips down.

The number of d c required to
cover the chains will much depend on
the individual worker; some people
work so much closer than others, but
the main thing is to get a firm even
line as a finish off.

**Spider Web Crochet.
Edging.**

An unusually fine and lacy design,
worked in Manlove's No. 100 Lace
Thread.

1st Row.—Make a row of chain the
length required.

2nd Row.—18 ch, 1 d c into 18th ch
of 1st row, 18 ch and another d c into
19th ch of 1st row. This forms a loop
of 18 ch and 1 d c into 36th ch of 1st
row, 18 ch and another d c into 36th
ch of 1st row of ch.

3rd Row.—Into each hanging loop
of 2nd row make 6 loops by crocheting
18 ch and making 1 d c into the loop
6 times. Connect 1 group of 6 loops
with the next by 16 ch fastened to
the 9th ch of the line of 18 ch into
the 2nd row with 2 d c and 16 ch and
1 d c into the next loop.

4th Row.—* Fasten the first loop
of the group of 6 loops to the line of
ch connecting the groups of loops in
the 3rd row by making 1 d c in the
9th ch of the loop and 1 d c into the

9th ch of the row of 16 ch of the
previous line, 7 ch, 1 d c into 2nd
loop, 18 ch, 1 d c into 2nd loop, 5 ch,
1 d c into 3rd loop, 18 ch, 1 d c into
3rd loop, 5 ch, 1 d c into 4th loop,
18 ch, 1 d c into 4th loop, 5 ch, 1 d c
into 5th loop, 18 ch, 1 d c into 5th
loop, 7 ch, 1 d c into 6th loop, 1 d c
into 9 ch of the row of 16 ch in the
previous line, 7 ch, 1 d c into 2nd
loop, 18 ch, 1 d c into 2nd loop, 7 ch,
1 d c into 3rd loop, 18 ch, 1 d c into
3rd loop, 9 ch, 1 d c into 4th loop,
1 d c into 9th ch of 1st loop of next
group, 9 ch, 1 d c into 2nd loop.
Repeat from *.

6th Row.—1 d c into 1st loop of 5th
row, 18 ch, 1 d c into 1st loop, 18 ch,
1 d c into 1st loop, 18 ch, 1 d c into
1st loop, 18 ch, 1 d c into 2nd loop,
18 ch, 1 d c into 2nd loop, 18 ch, 1 d c
into 2nd loop, 18 ch, 1 d c into 2nd
loop, 18 ch, 1 d c into 3rd loop. This
forms a group of 3 loops in each loop
of previous row, with a row of 18 ch
between each group.

7th Row.—1 d c into the 9th ch of
the 1st loops of the groups of three,
* 10 ch, 1 d c into 9th ch of the 2nd
group, 18 ch, 1 d c into the 2nd loop,
10 ch, 1 d c into 3rd loop, 1 d c into
9th ch of line of 18 ch in the previous
row, 1 d c into 1st ch of next group
of three, 10 ch, 1 d c into 2nd loop.
Repeat from * to the end of the row.

8th Row.—Make 1 d c into the 1st

loop of 7th row, * 18 ch, 1 d c into 1st loop, 18 ch, 1 d c into 1st loop, 18 ch, 1 d c into 1st loop, 18 ch, 1 d c into next loop. Repeat from *.

9th Row.—1 d c into 1st loop of 8th row, 10 ch, *, 1 d c into 2nd loop, 18 ch, 1 d c into 2nd loop, 18 ch, 1 d c into 2nd loop, 18 ch, 1 d c into 2nd loop, 10 ch, 1 d c into 3rd loop, 1 d c into 9th ch of line of 18 ch in the

11th Row.—1 d c into 1st loop of previous row, * 12 ch, 1 d c into 2nd loop, 18 ch, 1 d c into 2nd loop, 18 ch, 1 d c into 2nd loop, 18 ch, 1 d c into 2nd loop, 12 ch, 1 d c into 3rd loop, 1 d c into 9th ch of previous line of 18, 1 d c into 1st loop of next group. Repeat from *.

12th Row.—1 d c into 1st loop, * 1 d c into 2nd loop, 18 ch, 1 d c into 2nd

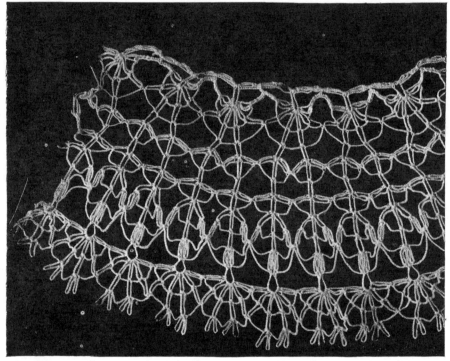

SPIDER WEB EDGING.

previous line, 1 d c into 9th ch of next loop, 10 ch, 1 d c into 2nd loop. Repeat from *.

10th Row.—Into the 1st loop of the group of 3 loops of the 9th row, make 1 d c, * 18 ch, 1 d c into the 1st loop, 10 ch, 1 d c into the 2nd loop, 18 ch, 1 d c into the 2nd loop, 10 ch, 1 d c into the 3rd loop, 18 ch, 1 d c into the 3rd loop, 18 ch, 1 d c into the 1st loop of next group of three. Repeat from *.

loop, 1 d c into 3rd loop, 16 ch, 1 d c into the 10th ch of preceding row, 16 ch, 1 d c into 1st loop of 2nd group. Repeat from *.

13th Row.—Into each loop of the 12th row make 6 loops of 18 ch each, connect one group of 6 loops with the next with a line of 18 ch.

14th Row.—Repeat the 4th row, as there is a line of 18 ch connecting the groups of loops in the previous line wherever a double is to be placed

26

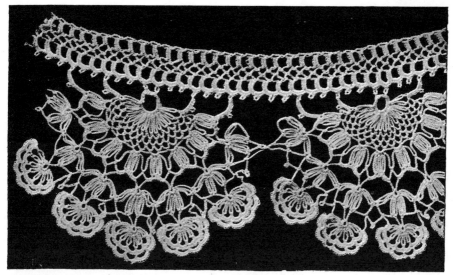

PANSY EDGING: A HANDSOME PATTERN FOR A TEA-CLOTH.

in the 9th ch of the previous 16 ch, in this row place a d c in the 10 ch of previous 18.

15*th Row*.—1 d c into 1st loop, * 9 ch, 1 d c into 2nd loop, 18 ch, 1 d c into 2nd loop, 18 ch, 1 d c into 2nd loop, 7 ch, 1 d c into 3rd loop, 18 ch, 1 d c into 3rd loop, 18 ch, 1 d c into 3rd loop, 9 ch, 1 d c into 4th loop, 1 d c into 1st loop of next group. Repeat from *.

Pansy Edging.

For this edging use Ardern's No. 40 Crochet Cotton. To make the insertion that is used for a heading ch 26 and join in a ring. Ch 6 and into the ring work 5 d c, 5 ch, 1 d c, 5 ch, 7 d c.

2*nd Row*.—Turn with 7 ch, 1 d c into first space in row below, 5 ch, 1 d c into second space, 5 ch and 1 d c into last space. (This end is the sewing-on side.)

3*rd Row*.—Turn with 5 ch, 5 d c into first space, 5 ch, 1 d c into second space, 5 ch, 7 d c into last space. Repeat from 2nd row.

The Scallops.

These are made after the required length of heading-insertion is finished, and each is completed before you proceed to the next scallop.

Ch 9, 1 d c into ninth picot along lower edge of insertion, ch 4, 1 d c into tenth picot, ch 11 and join to the first chain, so as to form a ring. Now make 16 loops of 18 ch each into the lowest part of the ring. After the sixteenth loop is made work d c around the remainder of the ring, including where it is joined to the picot loops. This gives the ring a firm appearance. When you have worked these d c round to the place where you started to make the first loop, ch 9 to lead up the side of the loop, and catch in top of loop ; * ch 5 and catch in top of next loop ; repeat from * till the loops are all united.

When you have come to the end of this row, which is the first row of the network, ch 10 and catch into the third picot from the one to which the central ring is joined. This makes a little "rope" to steady the work and unite it to the heading. Return back by making 5 d c, 5 ch and 5 d c over the 10 ch, the d c to come close together, so that the 5 ch between forms a picot. You are now back again at the first row of the network.

Turn with 5 ch and catch into first space in previous row, ch 5 and catch into next space; continue to end of row, and at the end of this row ch 10 and catch into the third picot. The next two rows are worked in precisely the same way (making 4 rows in all). This forms the network seen in the illustration below the long loops.

Into the first open space of the network make 3 loops of 18 ch each (all into the same space), then ch 18, and missing a space, catch into the third space in the network and proceed to make 3 loops of 18 ch each into the same space. Then with another 18 ch as a long "between loop," miss a space and catch into the fifth space of the network, and then make 3 loops into the same space.

Complete the row in this way: when finished you should have 8 groups of 3 loops each, and a long "between loop" in each case.

When you have reached the end of this row, ch 12 and catch into the third picot from where the last "rope" united the lace together.

Return with 6 d c, 6 ch, and 6 d c over the 12 ch which brings you back to the row of the loop just completed.

For the next row * 2 d c into the groups united in previous row, 4 d c over the upper end of the 8 ch in previous row. Then ch 10, catch back with a d c into the fourth ch from

the hook, 5 ch, 4 d c into chain in previous row, and repeat from *.

Into the little picot loop in previous row make six loops of 18 ch each, and ch 18 to carry you on to the next picot loop.

When the last loop is made, turn with 9 ch, make 1 d c into lower point of first loop of 18 ch, * ch 10, 1 d c into second loop, 1 d c into third loop, ch 10, catch back into fourth ch to form a picot, ch 5, 1 d c into fourth loop, 1 d c into fifth loop, ch 10 and catch the sixth loop into the centre of the 18 between chain in previous row, and also catch at the same place the first loop of next group. Repeat from *. Break thread at end of the last scallop.

Start the next row in the second of the picot loops, missing the upper group of loops with its centre picot. Into this second picot loop * make 7 loops of 12 ch each. After making the seventh loop, return with 6 ch, catch into bottom point of the last loop made, then ch 5 and catch into next loop; connect the seven loops in this way.

Turn, and fill in each of the 5 ch with 6 d c. When the other side of the little scallop is reached, turn again and make 7 ch over the top of each set of d c. Finally turn and fill these chains with 8 d c in each.

From the last of the 8 d c in the little scallop make 8 ch, catch into the 10 ch in row before; then ch 10, catch back into fourth to form a picot, ch 5, catch into 10 ch in row above, ch 10 and catch into next picot loops in previous row. Then proceed to make the second scallop by repeating from *. There are five little scallops around the lower edge of each of the large scallops

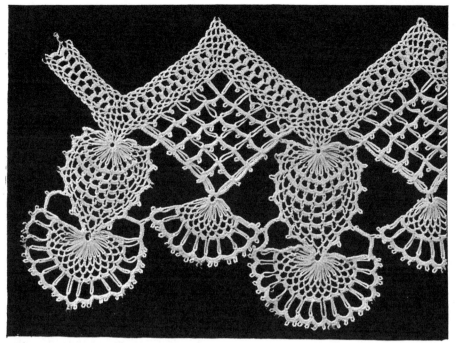

VANDYCK TRELLIS EDGING.

Vandyck Trellis Edging.

The narrow insertion used as a heading is made first, using Ardern's No. 40 Crochet Cotton. For this ch 30 and join in a ring.

1st Row.—6 ch, 1 d c into the ring, 6 ch, 5 d c into ring, 6 ch, 1 d c, 6 ch, 1 d c into ring.

2nd Row.—6 ch, 1 d c into first small space; 6 ch, 5 d c into next small space; 6 ch, 1 d c into space beyond the 5 d c in previous row; 6 ch, 1 d c into last space. Repeat these two rows ten times, *i.e.*, until a length of eleven double bars is worked.

After this, work six rows as follows: 6 ch, 1 d c into each space (in the first row passing over the 5 d c in previous row and making the d c into the space beyond). There should be four little loops in each row, and all the six rows are alike.

In order to produce the Vandyck effect a similar strip has now to be worked starting from the *side* of the strip just completed, as follows:— After completing the sixth row of little loops, as described above, make 6 ch and make 1 d c into the first loop along the edge (the illustration given just above will show what is meant), 6 ch, 5 d c into next loop, 6 ch, 1 d c into next loop, 6 ch, 1 d c into next loop.

Now go back to the beginning and repeat from the 2nd row.

The Vandyck heading is formed in this way, starting first at one side and then at the other of each strip, to secure the up-and-down pointed effect.

When this heading is the required length, start in the lowest point to work the first Cone, following the directions given for the Large Cone in a previous design.[1] At the apex

29

[1]Page 21.

For Advanced Workers.

work a Turkey Tail, also following the directions given on a previous page.[1]

For working the trellis that fills in the space between the cones, start in the fifth hole from the lower point of the Vandyck, chain 20, 1 d c into the same hole; ch 10, catch back into the 4th chain to form the picot; ch 5, 1 d c into the 7th hole; ch 20, 1 d c into the 7th hole; ch 10, catch back into 4th chain to form a picot; ch 5, 1 d c into 9th hole; ch 20, 1 d c into 9th hole; ch 10, picot, ch 5, 1 d c into 11th hole; ch 20, 1 d c into 11th hole; ch 10, picot, ch 5, 1 d c into 13th hole; ch 20, 1 d c into 13th hole; ch 10, 1 d c into 15th hole (which is the corner of the Vandyck).

Proceed in the same way to make loops and picots down the opposite edge of the Vandyck until the 5th hole from the lower point (where a cone starts) is reached.

2nd Row.—Ch 10, 1 d c into the 10th ch of the last loop made, * ch 8, 1 d c into the next loop in the previous row; repeat from * 3 times (making 4 times in all). This now brings us to the two loops in the upper corner. These have 1 d c into each (to unite them) without any intervening chain. Now proceed down the other side of the Vandyck, with 8 ch and 1 d c into each loop.

3rd Row.—* Ch 20, 1 d c back into the 1st ch; 4 d c over the 8 ch in the previous row; ch 7, 4 d c over the 8 ch. The d c are to come close together so that the 7 ch in the middle forms a little loop above the d c, like a picot. Proceed up and down the two sides of the Vandyck in this way, by repeating from *; when the upper corner is reached, however, omit the loop made by the 20 ch.

Repeat 2nd and 3rd row till 5 rows of open squares have been made. You should now be at the lower point of the trellis. On one side you have a row of 3 bars of 10 ch each; on the other side you have only a row of 2 bars (formed of the loops). Complete this side by working 10 ch and catching with a d c into the top of each loop. Now return, working 10 d c into the outside bar of 10 ch. Then form what looks like a picot by making 9 ch before starting the next 10 d c into the next bar. The first time this is done, catch the 5th ch of the 9 (forming the picot) into the top picot of the cone. At the lower point of the trellis make a small Turkey Tail, only having 10 loops to start with, instead of 16 as in the large Turkey Tail. The illustration shows very clearly where the tails and cones have to be united.

Four Edges in Venetian Crochet.

Top Design.

This lace is worked on a ch of the required length. Use Manlove's No. 80 Irish lace thread.

1st Row.—3 ch. 1 tr into every fourth ch.

2nd Row.—* 3 d c into each of next five spaces, 1 d c into next sp, turn, 1 ch 1 d c into each of next four second d c, turn, 1 d c into first sp, 1 ch 1 d c into each sp, turn, 1 d c into first sp, 1 ch, 1 d c into next sp, 1 ch 1 d c into next, turn, 1 d c into next sp, 1 ch 1 d c into next, slip-stitch down the side to the sp below, into which put 1 d c, turn and work d c closely around the pyramid, ending with a s into the next on foundation, turn, 10 ch, 1 d c into top of pyramid, 10 ch, 1 d c into the sp, 1 d c into next sp, turn, 15 d c over each 10 ch, turn, 1 d c into each d c all round, 2 d c into the sp, 2 d c into next sp, turn, 8 ch, 1 d c into sixth d c on the semicircle, turn back on the 8 ch and work 4 d c over the end, 8 ch, fasten to next fifth d c to the right, turn back on the 8 ch and put 4 d c over the end, 8 ch 1 d c into the d c over the tip of the pyramid, 8 ch, 1 d c into next fifth d c, 4 d c over the end of the 8 ch, 8 ch, 1 d c into fifth next d c, 4 d c over the end of the 8 ch, 5 ch, 1 d c into the third d c in first sp, turn and work d c closely over the ch all round, 1 d c into the sp, turn, 1 d c into each, 1 d c into second on first sp, turn, 1 d c into each to the sixth be-yond the top of figure, 10 ch, turn these back and fasten to the sixth d c to the right of the centre, turn, into the loop 3 d c, 5 ch, 5 d c, 5 ch, 5 d c, 8 ch, turn back to the right and fasten to the left side of the first picot on the loop, turn, into this top loop put 3 d c, 5 ch four times, end with 3 d c, 1 d c into first loop, 5 ch, 3 d c into loop, continue the d c down to the end, then repeat from *. The second mitre is connected with the first by two bars; the first of 5 ch with 3 d c, 5 ch, 3 d c worked over it is formed in the last row after the

first bar to the centre, and the second, between the next two bars, is of 10 ch, with 5 d c, 5 ch, 3 d c, 5 ch, 3 d c, 5 ch, 5 d c over it.

Second Design.

This, like the first, is worked on a length of ch.

1st Row.—3 ch, 1 tr into every fourth ch.

2nd Row.—3 d c into each of four sp, turn, 1 d c into each d c, * turn, miss first d c, 1 d c into each, and repeat from * until only 1 d c remains,

FOUR EDGES IN VENETIAN CROCHET.

A HANDSOME LACE IN 100 COTTON.

slip-stitch down to the first row on the right side, turn and work d c closely all round with a 5 ch picot after each third d c, 3 d c into each of next four sp, turn, 2 ch, 1 "knot" d c into each second d c, forming six sp. The "knot" d c is made as in the ordinary d c, but after forming the d c put the hook back through the loop just made and form another d c around the side of the loop, turn, * 1 d c into last loop, 3 ch, 1 d c into next, forming the knot on each d c, 2 ch, 1 d c into next and each sp to the end, * repeat until only one sp remains, then slip-stitch down the right side, turn and finish as in first pyramid, then repeat from the first *.

3rd Row.—12 ch, 1 d c into the top picot on each pyramid.

4th Row.—* 15 d c over the 12 ch, turn, 10 ch, 1 d c into the eighth d c, 10 ch, 1 d c into first d c, turn, into last loop 3 d c, 6 ch, 3 d c, 6 ch, 6 d c, 6 ch picot, 5 d c into next loop, 10 ch, turn and fasten to the d c after the second picot on first loop, turn, and into this top loop put 5 d c, 6 ch, 3 d c, 8 ch, 3 d c, 6 ch, 5 d c, into next loop 1 d c, 6 ch, 3 d c, 6 ch, 3 d c, * repeat over each 12 ch.

Third Design.

Start on a length of ch.

1st Row.—2 ch, 1 tr into every third ch.

2nd Row.—* 3 d c into each of three spaces, 1 d c into next sp, 8 ch, turn back and fasten over the tr to the right of the sp below, into the loop 5 d c, 5 ch, 5 d c, 2 d c into the sp, 1 d c into next sp, 15 ch, turn to the right and fasten to the second d c beyond the centre loop, turn, 25 d c over the ch, 2 d c into the sp, 1 d c into next sp, 2 ch 1 tr into every second d c on the semicircle, 2 ch, 1 d c into first d c on foundation. Turn, 2 d c into each of first five sp, 1 d c into next sp, 12 ch, turn the top round to the left and make a ring of first 6 ch, turn and put 10 d c into the ring, 6 d c into next 6 ch, 1 d c into the sp, 1 d c into next sp, 12 ch and repeat the ring and bar as in the last sp, 1 d c into the sp, 1 d c into next sp, 12 ch and repeat the ring and bar, 1 d c into the sp, 2 d c into each of next two sp, 7 ch, turn to the right and fasten to the fourth d c on the side of next bar, cross over the back of the bar with 1 ch and make a d c into the right side opposite the last, 3 ch, fasten to the fourth d c on bar to the right, cross over to the other side as before and make a d c, 3 ch, fasten to next bar and cross over as before, 7 ch, fasten to fourth d c on the right of the semicircle, turn, 4 d c, 6 ch, 4 d c over 7 ch, crossing at the back, 2 d c, 6 ch, 2 d c over each of next 3 ch, 4 d c, 6 ch, 4 d c over next ch, 2 d c into each sp to the end and 2 d c into the foundation sp, then repeat from *, connecting each semicircle to the preceding in the last row by a bar of 3 ch fastened after the second tr on the right side to the corresponding place on last semicircle.

Fourth Design.

Commence with a ring of 12 ch.

1st Row.—1 d c through each ch.

2nd Row.—2 d c into each d c.

3rd Row.—1 sp through first d c, 11 ch, 1 tr into third d c, 6 ch, 1 long tr into next third d c, 6 ch, 1 tr into next third d c, 6 ch, 1 long tr into next third d c, 6 ch, 1 tr into next third d c, 6 ch, 1 long tr into next third d c, 6 ch, 1 tr into next third d c, 6 ch, 1 d c into fifth of first 11 ch, * 8 d c into each of next 2 sp, turn and form a pyramid of d c, missing the first and last d c in each row until only one remains, then slip-stitch down the right side to the centre, turn and work d c closely all round and repeat from * three times. Each motif is joined to the preceding at the tip of a pyramid with a d c. When a sufficient length has been made, fill in the spaces at the top with * 1 d c into tip of first pyramid, working from left to right, 22 ch, turn the end down to the right and fasten to the twelfth ch, turn, 10 d c over one half of the ring, turn, 5 ch, 1 tr into

second d c, 2 ch 1 tr into each second d c on ring, 2 ch, 1 d c into tenth ch, turn, into each of next 2 sp put 2 d c, 6 ch, 2 d c, into next sp 2 d c, 8 ch, 1 d c into the centre of the 8 ch to form a picot, 4 ch, 1 d c into the centre of the side of the pyramid, 1 ch, 1 d c into last third, second and first ch, one 4 ch picot into side of last picot, 1 d c into each ch on the bar, 2 d c into the sp, repeat the bar with picots into the joining between the motifs, then 2 d c, the bar fastened to side of next pyramid, 2 d c in next sp, 2 d c, 6 ch, 2 d c into each of next 2 sp, 10 ch, 1 d c into top of next motif * and repeat.

Work a row of d c closely over the ch stitches, then a straightening row of 2 ch 1 tr into every third d c; finish with a row of 3 d c into each sp.

A Handsome Crochet Lace.

For this design use Manlove's No. 100 Lace Thread. The pine cones are made first, and the fan-shaped leaves are afterwards inserted.

Form 16 ch into a ring into which put 9 loops of 18 ch each.

2nd Row.—9 ch to turn, 6 ch into each loop, turn and slip-stitch to top of first loop, 6 ch into each loop, and repeat this row until there is only one loop, into which put 8 ch, 6 d c into each loop down the side to the ring, d c into ring to opposite side of the cone, then up the side to the top as at the other side, then into the 8 ch form another cone in the same way. A third cone is formed in the tip of the second, and in this put 10 ch in the final loop, into which two cones are inserted for the lower edge. Repeat these five cones in strips, and connect them at the tip of opposite cones in the edge.

For Advanced Workers.

For the fan-shaped leaves make 12 ch, form into a ring, 38 ch, form last 16 into a ring, 34 ch, form 12 into a ring, into this ring 3 ch, 6 tr, 5 ch, 2 tr, 5 ch, 6 tr, 3 ch, 1 d c, 18 ch, 1 d c into the 16 ch ring, 16 loops of 18 c h each into the ring, 18 ch and work into the third ring as the first, 16 ch, 1 d c over the 10th of the 22 ch, 1 d c over corresponding stitch of the other 22 ch, 16 ch, 1 d c into the 3 ch on the 1st ring, 5 ch, 6 d c into next space, 24 ch, 6 d c into next space, 5 ch, 1 d c into the last 3 ch, 18 d c over next 18 ch, 9 ch, 1 d c into top of first loop on ring, 6 ch into each loop around, turn, 6 ch into each 6 ch loop, turn, 6 d c over each 6 ch loop, 18 d c over the 18 ch, then work around the third ring as the first, fastening to the ring in the top cone at the left side in the centre of the 24 ch, fasten at the opposite side in the same way and connect the lower leaf with three bars of ch and d c as in the illustration. For the heading work 5 d c over the 5 ch on the side of the connecting figure, 18 ch, d c over ring of cone, 18 ch, d c over next 5 ch, 18 ch, 1 d c over 10th of next 22 ch and 1 d c over same place on next 22 ch, 18 ch, and repeat from the beginning.

Second top row, * 4 tr before 5 d c, 6 ch, 4 tr after the 5 d c, 16 ch, 4 long tr into ring of cone, 16 ch and repeat from *.

Finish with a row of d c.

Venetian Crochet Lace.

This design is easily worked, and is suitable for trimming blouses or forming yokes, collars, etc. It also makes a lovely border for handkerchiefs, and if worked in coarser linen thread is charming for tea-cloth, tray-cloth, or d'oily edging and insertion.

For the lace, use very fine crochet thread, Manlove's No. 80 Irish lace thread will do, and a very fine crochet-hook. Form 8 ch into a ring, into which put 24 d c, 1 d c into the first d c on ring.

1st Row.—4 ch, 2 long tr into the first d c on ring, retaining the last loop on the needle, then work off all the loops together, * 5 ch, 3 long tr into next third d c on ring, working the tr in the same way as the last. Repeat from * six times.

2nd Row.—5 ch, 6 d c into first loop. 6 ch, 6 d c into same loop, * into the next loop put 6 d c, 6 ch, 6 d c, 6 d c into next loop, 10 ch, turn these back, and fasten to the d c to the left of the last picot, turn, and into the 10 ch loop put 6 d c, 6 ch, 3 d c, 6 ch, 3 d c, 6 ch, 6 d c, 1 d c into the loop below, 6 ch, 6 d c into the same loop, repeat from * three times, slip-stitching up the last 6 d c.

The motifs are connected in the centre of each of the three picots at opposite sides, the spaces between, at the lower edge, are filled in with three loops corresponding to the three at each side of the motif.

To fill the space at the top, fasten the thread to the first of the three picots at the right-hand side of the space, make a chain sufficiently long to cross over to the opposite picot at the left evenly, turn and work d c over the chain 18 times, 8 ch, fasten back to the twelfth d c, and into this loop work 11 d c, 6 d c over the ch stitches, turn and work three groups of tr same as into the centre of motif, fastening the last 5 ch to the sixth d c on ch, turn, and work round as in the last row on motif, connecting to the motifs below in the three centre picots as before.

Break off the thread, and fill in each space in the same way, then work a row of 1 tr, 5 ch at the top, spacing the tr so that the ch stitches form an even line with the last row, and putting a tr into each picot. Finish with a row of d c worked closely into each space.

Insertion to match is made by filling in the spaces at both sides as at the top of the lace, and then working the straightening lines.

Edging for Blinds or Valance.

Use Strutt's Belper Super Crochet Cotton, No. 18. Sp = a space ; which is made by working 2 ch and missing 2.

Make 100 ch for foundation.

1st Row.—Miss 8 ch and work 4 tr in next 4 ch, make 2 sp by * missing 2 ch and working 2 ch, 1 tr in next ch.

Repeat from *. 3 tr, 22 sp, 4 tr, miss 2 ch, 3 ch, 1 d c in next, 3 ch, miss 2 and 4 tr in last 4 ch.

2nd Row.—3 ch, 3 tr, 5 ch, 4 tr, 2 sp, 4 tr, 1 sp, 16 tr on 5 sp, 1 sp, 16 tr, 1 sp, 10 tr, 4 sp, 7 tr.

3rd Row.—8 ch, 7 tr, 4 sp, 4 tr, 1 sp, 4 tr, 3 sp, 4 tr, 1 sp, 4 tr, 3 sp, 4 tr, 1 sp, 4 tr, 2 sp, 4 tr, 3 ch, 1 d c, 3 ch. 4 tr.

4th Row.—3 ch, 3 tr, 5 ch, 4 tr, 2 sp, 4 tr, 1 sp, 10 tr, 1 sp, 4 tr, 1 sp, 10 tr, 1 sp. 4 tr, 1 sp, 10 tr, 1 sp 7 tr.

5th Row.—15 ch, 3 tr in the 3 furthest from needle, 4 tr, 2 sp, 4 tr, 3 sp, 4 tr, 1 sp, 4 tr, 3 sp, 4 tr, 1 sp, 4 tr, 3 sp, 4 tr, 2 sp, 4 tr, 3 ch, 1 d c, 3 ch, 4 tr.

6th Row.—3 ch, 3 tr, 5 ch, 4 tr, 2 sp, 16 tr, 1 sp, 16 tr, 1 sp, 16 tr, 4 sp, 7 tr.

7th Row.—9 ch, 3 tr in the 3 ch farthest from needle and 1 on nearest of the 7 tr, 3 ch, 1 d c on 4th tr, 3 ch, 4 tr in space, 22 sp, 4 tr, 3 ch, 1 d c, 3 ch, 4 tr.

8th Row.—3 ch, 3 tr, 5 ch, 4 tr, 2 sp, 61 tr, 1 sp, 4 tr, 5 ch, 4 tr.

9th Row.—8 ch, 4 tr, 3 ch, 1 d c, 3 ch, 1 tr, 1 sp, 4 tr, 1 sp, 58 tr, 2 sp, 4 tr, 3 ch, 1 d c, 3 ch, 4 tr.

10th Row.—3 ch, 3 tr, 5 ch, 4 tr, 2 sp, 10 tr, 10 ch, 16 tr, 10 ch, 16 tr, 10 ch, 10 tr, 1 sp, 10 tr, 5 ch, 4 tr.

11th Row.—8 ch, 4 tr, 3 ch, 1 d c, 3 ch, 4 tr, 1 sp, 4 tr, 1 sp, 7 tr, 5 ch, 3 d c, 5 ch, 10 tr, 5 ch, 3 d c, 5 ch, 10 tr, 3 d c, 5 ch, 7 tr, 2 sp, 4 tr, 3 ch, 1 d c, 3 ch, 4 tr.

12th Row.—3 ch, 3 tr, 5 ch, 4 tr, 2 sp, 4 tr, 4 ch, 5 d c, 4 ch, 4 tr, 4 ch, 5 d c, 4 ch, 4 tr, 4 ch, 5 d c, 4 ch, 4 tr, 1 sp, 10 tr, 5 ch, 7 tr.

13th Row.—8 ch, 7 tr, 3 ch, 1 d c, 3 ch, 4 tr, 1 sp, 4 tr, 1 sp, 4 tr, 4 ch, 5 d c, 4 ch, 4 tr, 4 ch, 5 d c, 4 ch, 4 tr, 4 ch, 5 d c, 4 ch, 4 tr. 2 sp, 4 tr, 3 ch, 1 d c, 3 ch, 4 tr.

VENETIAN CROCHET EDGING.

For Advanced Workers.

14*th Row.*—3 ch, 3 tr, 5 ch, 4 tr, 2 sp, 4 tr, 6 ch, 3 d c, 6 ch, 4 tr, 6 ch, 3 d c, 6 ch, 4 tr, 6 ch, 3 d c, 6 ch, 4 tr, 1 sp, 10 tr, 5 ch, 7 tr.

15*th Row.*—5 ch, 4 tr, 3 ch, 1 d c, 3 ch, 4 tr, 1 sp, 4 tr, 1 sp, 7 tr, 6 ch, 1 d c, 6 ch, 10 tr, 6 ch, 1 d c, 6 ch, 10 tr, 6 ch, 1 d c, 6 ch, 7 tr, 2 sp, 4 tr, 3 ch, 1 d c, 3 ch, 4 tr.

16*th Row.*—3 ch, 3 tr, 5 ch, 4 tr, 2 sp, 10 tr, 2 ch, 16 tr, 2 ch, 16 tr, 2 ch, 10 tr, 1 sp, 10 tr, 5 ch, 4 tr.

17*th Row.*—5 ch, 4 tr, 3 ch, 1 d c, 3 ch, 1 tr (on 4th), 1 sp, 4 tr, 1 sp, 58 tr, 2 sp, 4 tr, 3 ch, 1 d c, 3 ch, 4 tr.

23*rd Row.*—15 ch, 3 tr in 3 ch farthest from needle, 4 tr on 4, 2 sp, 4 tr, 3 sp, 4 tr, 1 sp, 4 tr, 3 sp, 4 tr, 1 sp, 4 tr, 3 sp, 4 tr, 2 sp.

24*th Row.*—2 sp, 16 tr, 1 sp, 16 tr, 1 sp, 16 tr, 4 sp, 7 tr.

25*th Row.*—10 ch, 3 tr on 3 ch, 1 tr on tr, 3 ch, 1 d c on 4th tr, 3 ch, 4 tr in space, 20 sp.

26*th Row.*—16 tr, 1 sp, 43 tr, 1 sp, 4 tr, 5 ch, 4 tr.

27*th Row.*—8 ch, 4 tr on 4, 3 ch, 1 d c, 3 ch, 1 tr, 1 sp, 4 tr, 1 sp, 40 tr, 1 sp, 4 tr, 1 sp, 4 tr.

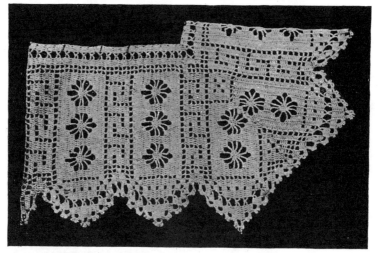

AN EDGING FOR A BLIND OR VALANCE.

18*th Row.*—3 ch, 3 tr, 5 ch, 4 tr, 2 sp, 61 tr, 1 sp, 4 tr, 5 ch, 4 tr.

19*th Row.*—5 ch, 4 tr, 3 ch, 1 d c, 3 ch, 4 tr, 22 sp, 4 tr, 3 ch, 1 d c, 3 ch, 4 tr.

To Turn the Corner.

20*th Row.*—4 tr, 5 ch, 4 tr, 2 sp, 4 tr, 1 sp, 16 tr, 1 sp, 16 tr, 1 sp, 10 tr, 4 sp.

21*st Row.*—8 ch, 7 tr, 4 sp, 4 tr, 1 sp, 4 tr, 3 sp, 4 tr, 1 sp, 4 tr, 3 sp, 4 tr, 1 sp, 4 tr, 2 sp, 4 tr.

22*nd Row.*—4 tr, 2 sp, 4 tr. 1 sp, 10 tr, 1 sp, 4 tr, 1 sp, 10 tr, 1 sp, 10 tr, 1 sp, 10 tr, 1 sp. 7 tr.

28*th Row.*—1 sp, 7 tr, 1 sp, 10 tr, 10 ch, 16 tr, 10 ch, 10 tr, 1 sp, 10 tr, 5 ch, 4 tr.

29*th Row.*—8 ch, 4 tr, 3 ch, 1 d c, 3 ch, 4 tr, 1 sp, 4 tr, 1 sp, 7 tr, 5 ch, 3 d c, 5 ch, 10 tr, 5 ch, 3 d c, 5 ch, 7 tr, 1 sp, 4 tr.

30*th Row.*—4 tr, 1 sp, 4 tr, 5 ch, 5 d c, 5 ch, 4 tr, 5 ch, 5 d c, 5 ch, 4 tr, 1 sp, 10 tr, 5 ch, 7 tr.

31*st Row.*—8 ch, 7 tr, 3 ch, 1 d c, 3 ch, 4 tr, 1 sp, 4 tr, 1 sp, 4 tr, 5 ch, 5 d c, 5 ch, 4 tr, 5 ch, 5 d c, 5 ch, 1 tr.

36

32nd Row.—4 tr, 6 ch, 3 d c, 6 ch, 4 tr, 6 ch, 3 d c, 6 ch, 4 tr, 1 sp, 10 tr, 5 ch, 7 tr.

33rd Row.—5 ch, 4 tr, 3 ch, 1 d c, 3 ch, 4 tr, 1 sp, 4 tr, 1 sp, 7 tr, 6 ch, 1 d c, 6 ch, 13 tr, 6 ch, 1 d c, 6 ch, 1 tr in loop.

34th Row.—4 tr in loop, 2 ch, 16 tr, 2 ch, 10 tr, 1 sp, 10 tr, 5 ch, 4 tr.

35th Row.—5 ch, 4 tr, 3 ch, 1 d c, 3 ch, 1 tr, 1 sp, 4 tr, 1 sp, 28 tr.

36th Row.—31 tr, 1 sp, 4 tr, 5 ch, 4 tr.

37th Row.—5 ch, 4 tr, 3 ch, 1 d c, 3 ch, 4 tr, 8 sp.

38th Row.—22 tr in 7 sp, 2 sp, 7 tr.

39th Row.—8 ch, 4 tr, 3 sp, 4 tr, 1 sp, 4 tr.

40th Row.—1 sp. 7 tr, 3 sp, 4 tr.

41st Row.—5 ch, 4 tr, 2 sp, 4 tr.

42nd Row.—4 tr, 2 sp, 4 tr.

43rd Row.—5 ch, 4 tr.

44th Row.—11 ch, 4 tr in chain farthest from needle, 2 ch, join to treble at side, slipstitch along side of tr.

45th Row.—2 sp, 4 tr.

46th Row.—8 ch, 4 tr, 2 sp, 4 tr on side of tr, 2 ch, join to make space.

47th Row.—Slipstitch along space at side, 7 tr, 3 sp, 4 tr.

48th Row.—15 ch, 4 tr on 4, 3 sp, 4 tr, 1 sp, 4 tr, 2 ch. Join.

49th Row.—Slipstitch along the 4 tr at side, 18 tr, 2 sp, 7 tr.

50th Row.—11 ch, 4 tr in ch farthest from needle, 3 ch, 1 d c, 3 ch, 1 tr, 10 more sp.

51st Row.—Tr in 9 sp, 1 sp, 4 tr, 5 ch, 4 tr.

52nd Row.—8 ch, 4 tr on 4, 3 ch, 1 d c, 3 ch, 1 tr, 1 sp, 4 tr, 1 sp, 31 tr on tr, join 20 ch.

53rd Row.—Slipstitch along 4 tr, 10 ch, miss 2 tr, 16 tr, 10 ch, 10 tr, 1 sp, 10 tr, 5 ch, 4 tr.

54th Row.—8 ch, 4 tr, 3 ch, 1 d c, 3 ch, 4 tr, 1 sp, 4 tr, 1 sp, 7 tr, 5 ch, 3 d c, 5 ch, 10 tr, 5 ch, 3 d c, 5 ch, 4 tr in next long loop of chain. Join.

55th Row.—Slipstitch along tr at side, 5 ch, 5 d c, 5 ch, 4 tr, 5 ch, 5 d c, 5 ch, 4 tr, 1 sp, 4 tr, 1 sp, 4 tr, 5 ch, 7 tr.

56th Row.—8 ch, 7 tr, 3 ch, 1 d c, 3 ch, 4 tr, 1 sp, 4 tr, 1 sp, 4 tr, 5 ch, 5 d c, 5 ch, 4 tr, 5 ch, 5 d c, 5 ch, 4 tr, 1 sp.

57th Row.—1 sp, 4 tr, 6 ch, 3 d c, 6 ch, 4 tr, 6 ch, 3 d c, 6 ch, 4 tr, 1 sp, 13 tr, 5 ch, 7 tr.

58th Row.—5 ch, 4 tr, 3 ch, 1 d c, 3 ch, 4 tr, 1 sp, 4 tr, 1 sp, 7 tr, 6 ch, 1 d c, 6 ch, 10 tr, 6 ch, 1 d c, 6 ch, 7 tr, 1 sp, 4 tr, 1 sp. Join.

59th Row.—7 tr, 1 sp, 10 tr, 2 ch, 16 tr, 2 ch, 10 tr, 1 sp, 10 tr, 5 ch, 4 tr.

60th Row.—5 ch, 4 tr, 3 ch, 1 d c, 3 ch, 1 tr, 1 sp, 4 tr, 1 sp, 40 tr, 1 sp, 4 tr, 1 sp, 4 tr, 1 sp.

61st Row.—13 tr, 1 sp, 43 tr, 1 sp, 4 tr, 5 ch, 4 tr.

62nd Row.—5 ch, 4 tr, 3 ch, 1 d c, 3 ch, 4 tr, 21 sp.

63rd Row.—1 sp, 16 tr, 1 sp, 16 tr, 1 sp, 16 tr, 4 sp, 7 tr.

64th Row.—8 ch, 7 tr, 2 sp, 4 tr, 3 sp, 4 tr, 1 sp, 4 tr, 3 sp, 4 tr, 1 sp, 4 tr, 3 sp, 4 tr, 2 sp, 4 tr. Join.

65th Row.—Slipstitch along side of treble the length of 3 sp, then along the 5 ch, then 3 ch, 1 d c in tr, 3 ch, 4 tr, 2 sp, 4 tr, remainder as 22nd row.

66th Row.—As 21st row, except at the top when 4 tr on 4, 2 sp, 4 tr, 5 ch, 4 tr.

This finishes the corner.

For Advanced Workers.

A Lovely Lace for D'oilies.

This is also useful for collars or dress trimming. For very fine lacy work use No. 100 cotton. It looks very well, however, in Ardern's No. 40, or even coarser. We give the directions for working in a very fine cotton; but if a coarser thread is used, the long chains should not be more than 14 in number, and the short ones a trifle less than those given below.

For Manlove's 100 thread, use a fine hook. 18 ch, and join in a ring. Into this make 16 loops of 22 ch each. Then go up the side of last loop with 11 ch. Catch into top of loop 5 ch, and catch into next loop with a d c. Complete row in this way. Turn and continue making this network by working to and fro till there is only 5 ch left at the tip of the cone.

Into the tip make 3 loops of 18 ch each; then ch 18 and catch into next little jutting loop at the side of the cone. Fill each in the same way with 3 loops of 18 ch.

When you come to the last loop on that side at the broad base of the cone, make enough ch to go down to the stem part. Into that make 7 d c, 7 ch, 7 d c up the side of the first set of loops with 11 ch. This brings you to the opposite side of the cone. Into this work groups of 3 loops of 18 ch each, with 18 ch between, as you did on the opposite side. Break off at the top.

Starting with the first group nearest stem on right hand side, make 1 d c into each loop, keeping the three close together. Ch 8, catch into centre of the 18 ch below, 8 ch, and d c into next set of loops. Complete row in this way.

Now into the top of the first group of loops caught together make 2 d c, then 4 d c into the 8 ch below, 10 ch, catch back so as to form a picot into fourth ch, 5 ch, 4 d c into opposite side.

The first cone is worked complete all the way round; the others join at the first three, or the last three picots in the row just described.

To make the outer edge. Into the little loop made by the picot at the top of the cone and into the three picots each side of it, make 6 loops of 18 ch each, with 18 ch between each set. Between each cone, and up to the remaining picot, make 14 ch, then 5 ch across to opposite side and so on.

2nd Row.—Catch a loop from each set down to the between ch, with 1 d c in each. 10 ch to next 2 loops, 1 d c to each. Make a picot chain (10 ch, catch back to fourth to form picot, 5 ch) to the next two loops, 10 ch to last loop, and carry down to between ch.

Between the cones, take down the last loop against the 14 ch, fill with d c, and put 5 d c over the 5 ch. Up the other side to match.

3rd Row.—Into each of the picots make 7 loops of 12 each. Go up the side of the last loop with 6 ch, catching across to each loop with 5 ch between.

Turn and fill in with d c. Before turning catch into the ch that is near.

From the last, 5 d c, 8 ch, 1 d c into next space of ch. Make a picot ch to next space of ch, and 10 ch up, and proceed to fill in picots on next cone.

The last picot on one cone and the first on the next are caught together to lessen any fulness.

For the sewing-on edge, make a straightening ch, and fill in with d c.

Pagoda Edging.

This edging can be worked in Ardern's crochet cotton No. 40 or coarser.

A ring of 12 ch.

1st Row.—6 ch, 3 tr, 5 ch, 3 tr, 3 ch, 1 tr into ring.

2nd Row.—6 ch, 3 tr into first sp, 7 ch, 1 d c into second sp, 7 ch, 3 tr, 3 ch, 1 tr into last sp.

A LOVELY LACE FOR D'OILIES.

3rd Row.—6 ch, 3 tr, 7 ch, 1 d c into next sp, 7 ch, 1 d c into next, 7 ch, 3 tr, 3 ch, 1 tr into last sp.

4th Row.—6 ch, 3 tr into sp, 7 ch, 1 d c into next, 7 ch, 3 tr, 5 ch, 3 tr into centre sp, 7 ch, 1 d c into next sp, 7 ch, 3 tr, 3 ch, 1 tr into last sp.

5th Row.—6 ch, 3 tr into sp, 7 ch, 1 d c into next sp, 7 ch, 3 tr into sp, 7 ch, 1 d c into 5 ch between the groups of 3 tr, 7 ch, 3 tr into sp, 7 ch, 1 d c into next sp, 7 ch, 3 tr, 3 ch, 1 tr into last sp.

6th Row.—6 ch, 3 tr into sp, 7 ch, 1 d c into next sp, 7 ch, 3 tr into next, 7 ch, 1 d c into sp, 7 ch, 1 d c into sp, 7 ch, 3 tr into next, 7 ch, 1 d c into sp, 7 ch, 3 tr, 3 ch, 1 tr into last sp.

7th Row.—6 ch, 3 tr, 7 ch, 1 d c, 7 ch, 3 tr, 7 ch, 1 d c, 7 ch, 3 tr, 5 ch, 3 tr into middle sp, 7 ch, 1 d c, 7 ch, 3 tr, 7 ch, 1 d c, 7 ch, 3 tr, 3 ch, 1 tr.

8th Row.—6 ch, 3 tr, * 7 ch, 1 d c, 7 ch, 3 tr. Repeat from * four times, 3 ch, 1 tr into same sp as last 3 tr.

9th Row.—6 ch, 3 tr, 7 ch, 1 d c, 7 ch, 3 tr, 7 ch, 1 d c, 7 ch, 3 tr, 7 ch, 1 d c, 7 ch, 1 d c, 7 ch, 3 tr, 7 ch, 1 d c, 7 ch, 1 d c, 7 ch, 3 tr, 7 ch, 1 d c, 7 ch, 3 tr, 3 ch, 1 tr.

10th Row.—6 ch, 3 tr, * 7 ch, 1 d c, 7 ch, 3 tr. Repeat from * twice, 5 ch,

3 tr into same sp as last 3 tr, * 7 ch, 1 d c, 7 ch, 3 tr. Repeat from * twice, 3 ch, 1 tr into same sp.

For next fan commence in 7 ch, right side of 3 tr, 5 ch, 3 tr of 10th row.

Each strip is joined in last row.

There are three fans in strip.

1st Row.—Catch cotton into the 5 ch between the groups of 3 tr of last fan, 12 ch, 1 s c into same, 5 ch to form a ring.

2nd Row.—Make 12 loops of 16 ch into ring.

3rd Row.—8 ch, 1 d c into top of first loop, * 7 ch, 1 d c. Repeat from * 10 times.

4th Row.—7 ch, * 3 tr into 7 ch, 7 ch, 1 d c into next 7 ch. Repeat from * to end; the last space should have 3 tr.

5th Row.—7 ch, 1 d c into sp, 7 ch, 3 tr into next. Repeat to end.

6th Row.—Same as 5th row.

7th Row.—9 ch, 3 tr, 7 ch, 1 d c; * 7 ch, 3 tr, 7 ch, 1 d c. Repeat from * to end, but work 9 ch before last d c.

8th Row.—Make 12 loops of 16 ch into 9 ch. Turn.

9th Row.—8 ch, 1 d c into top of first loop, * 7 ch, 1 d c. Repeat from * to end of loops.

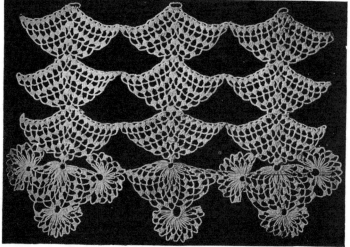

PAGODA EDGING.

10th Row.—4 ch, 3 tr into first sp, * 7 ch, 1 d c, 7 c h, 3 tr. Repeat from * to end of small fan. Now continue along last row of large fan. 7 ch, miss 7 ch, 3 tr, 3 tr into next 7 ch, 7 ch, 1 d c, 7 ch, 3 tr, 7 ch, 1 d c. Into same sp as last d c make 12 loops of 18 ch. Continue to make another small fan. When small fan is completed, work again into large fan as follows :—7 ch, miss 7 ch, 1 d c, 1 d c into next ch, 7 ch, 3 tr, 7 ch, 1 d c, 7 ch, 1 d c into the 9 ch. Into this 9 ch work another small fan. Both small fans at side should be caught to large fan above when working last row.

The bottom fan of centre strip in illustration is worked in the same way, but the two side fans are omitted.

Star Border for a Tea-Cloth.

Form 18 ch into a ring, 6 ch, 2 d c into the ring 12 times.

2nd Row.—5 ch, 1 d c into each loop.

3rd Row.—3 d c, 5 ch, 3 d c into each loop.

4th Row.—Slipstitch to first picot, 1 d c into it, * 14 ch, 1 d c into it 4

times, 5 ch, 1 d c into next picot, 5 ch, 1 d c into next picot, then into same picot, repeat from *, closing the circle with 5 ch, 1 d c.

5th Row.—1 d c after the last picot, 5 ch, 1 d c into top of first loop, 6 ch, 1 d c into each of next 3 loops, 5 ch, 1 d c over the next 5 ch beside the picot, * repeat.

6th Row.—5 d c over each 5 ch, 3 d c, 5 ch, 3 d c over each 6 ch.

The motifs are connected in corresponding picots after the manner illustrated.

Heading.

1st Row.—* 2 tr into first picot, 20 ch, 2 tr into next picot, 5 ch, 1 d c into next picot, 5 ch, 2 tr into next picot, 20 ch, 2 tr into next picot, 2 ch, repeat from *.

2nd Row.—* 2 tr over centre of 20 ch, 10 ch, 2 tr into next 2 tr, 5 ch, 2 tr into the d c, 5 ch, 2 tr into the next trs, 10 ch, 2 tr over centre of the 20 ch, cross over to centre of next 20 ch and repeat from *.

3rd Row.—Work d c closely over the stitches in last row.

Mignonette Border.

With No. 42 crochet cotton make 18 ch, 1 d c into first ch, 9 ch, 1 d c into end of loop, into the side of the last d c put * 4 loops of 18 ch each, 9 ch, 1 d c into top of last loop, 2 loops of 18 ch each into last d c, these two loops are on the opposite side to the

three at the
other side of
the three
horizontal
chains, 18 ch
1 d c into last
d c, 9 ch, 1
d c into top
of loop, then
into side
of last d c
repeat from *

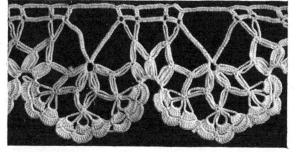

MIGNONETTE BORDER.

beginning
over each
mitre.

At the top
side * collect
the four
groups of
loops con-
tained in the
mitre with a
d c through
each loop, 20

ad lib., according to the length of
the edging required.

At the lower edge * 7 tr into each of
the first three loops, 7 tr into each of
next three loops, 7 tr into each of next
three loops, 1 d c into each loop of
next three groups of 3 loops, * repeat.

2nd Row.—Fasten the thread to the
first d c before a mitre to the left
and make 8 ch, 1 d c between each
of the group of trs, turn, * 7 ch,
8 tr, 1 d c into first 8 ch, 8 tr, 1 d c
into each of next two 8 ch, *
repeat twice more, then from the

ch, 1 d c into next loop, 6 ch, 1 d c into
next loop, 10 ch, 1 d c into next, 6 ch,
1 d c into next, 20 ch, 1 d c into next,
then repeat from *.

2nd Row.—Work d c closely over
the chs, closing in a ring over the
centre loops, form a 5 ch picot over
each loop.

3rd Row.—* 2 tr into first picot after
the 20 ch, 5 ch, 2 tr into next picot,
10 ch, 2 tr into next picot, 5 ch, 2 tr
into next picot, 12 ch, *, repeat.

4th Row.—d c closely into each
space.

STAR BORDER FOR A TEA CLOTH.

IRISH CROCHET.

ONE OF THE LATEST DESIGNS IN IRISH CROCHET.

One of the Latest Designs in Irish Crochet.

This beautiful design in Irish crochet lace with insertion to match is quite easily and quickly made. The model has been worked in No. 24 crochet cotton in order to show the stitches distinctly, but for practical purposes Manlove's No. 60 Irish lace thread will be found the most satisfactory, though if a very fine lace be preferred No. 80 in the same thread will be required. Any coarse cotton or linen thread will answer for padding. Use a No. 6 crochet hook for the No. 60, or a No. 7 for the finer thread.

A great deal depends on how the centre is worked, as the whole design starts from this, and a good firm centre tends to make firm the surrounding work, and makes it easier to add the "filling."

Take about a yard of coarse thread for padding, fold in two, insert the crochet hook in the fold and fasten the crochet thread with a double stitch; now twist the padding round from left to right to form a ring with the end of the padding overlapping, thus starting a ring of double padding for the centre. Over both work 16 double stitches. Pull the end of the padding to close the ring, and make it as small as possible; make a single stitch through the first on the ring, then over the padding work a double stitch into each on the ring.

In the third row put 2 d c into each of second row.

In the fourth row work 1 d c into each of preceding.

Leave the padding depending, 1 d c into next stitch, 5 ch, 1 tr into next d c, then 2 ch, 1 tr, into each of next 10 d c.

Turn, 5 ch, 1 tr into second tr of preceding row, 2 ch 1 tr into each tr, 2 ch 1 tr into the third of the 5 ch, slip stitch down 3 to the padding, which take up, and turning back work 3 d c over it into last space, 3 d c into next space, * 20 d c over the padding alone, twist round, downwards from left to right and bring the end over the first space in last row and work two more double stitches into this space, 3 d c into next space, 1 d c into next, and repeat from * until 7 loops are formed, 3 d c down the side of last space. Fasten off the padding on the back and cut away the superfluous thread.

Fasten thread to first stitch on the centre, before this top portion, and work 5 picot loops over the space, each loop made thus:—9 ch, form 6 of these into a picot by inserting the hook through the third ch and pulling the thread through it and that on the needle, 4 ch, fasten this loop to third next stitch. After the fifth loop make half another, as far as one stitch after the picot ; fasten this to the fourth d up the side of the top piece.

Turn back, work another loop into each of the five, and fasten the last one into the side of the first loop on the top piece, slip stitch up three on the loop and make a d c into it, turn back and put a loop into last loop, 9 ch, fasten with 1 d c to next loop, turn back on this ch and work 9 d c over it, turn again, miss the first d c, 1 d c into next, 1 tr into each d c, 1 d c over the first ch, make three loops into

next three, and form another group of tr into a 9 ch loop as before.

Continue working the loops all round, putting one into each of the loops on the top, and fasten one at the beginning, into the centre and at the end of each group of tr. Work another row and put the group of tr between the two loops over the preceding group. This completes the motif.

When several have been made, join together by picot loops, working half a loop from side to side, as in the illustration.

When all are joined make the " straightening line " at the top, consisting of trs separated by 3 ch, 1 tr at each side of a picot. Then along the top work a row of 4 d into each space.

Work a similar row at the lower edge, making a double stitch between the mitres, instead of the tr, then over this "straightening line" work * 5 d c into each of next two spaces, 8 ch, 1 d c into the centre of these 10 d c, turning backwards, 8 ch 1 d c into first of 10 d c, turn, 3 d c into last loop, 6 ch 7 d c into same loop, 5 d c into next loop, 8 ch, turn back and fasten to the fifth d c of preceding loop, turn again and into this top loop put 3 d c, 6 ch 3 d c, 6 ch 3 d c, 6 ch 3 d c. Then down the side of next loop work 2 d c 6 ch 3 d c, into next space on the " straightening line " put 2 d c 6 ch 2 d c, and repeat from * all round.

In the insertion the motifs are reversed and joined in a similar

INSERTION TO MATCH THE LACE.

Irish Crochet.

IRISH CROCHET VENETIAN LACE.

manner, the "straightening line" is worked at both sides, and a second row worked into the first, putting the trs into those below, and finishing with a row of double stitches.

Irish Crochet Venetian Lace in Linen Thread.

This beautiful lace is suitable for table lingerie, and can be very easily made, as it requires little or no filling, the motifs being joined together in the making. It is practically everlasting, and of course the most expensive of all Irish crochet.

For this sample Barbour's F.D.A. Linen Crochet Thread No. 60, with No. 12 for padding, was used. A fine crochet hook is necessary, and there must be no uneven or loose stitches, as this would spoil the effect. Wind the padding thread around the tip of the thumb ten times, work 112 double stitches into this large ring, then over a single padding thread work double stitch half way round, 10 d c over the padding alone, fasten with a d c into the next d c on the ring,

25 d c over the padding and fasten into the same stitch, 20 d c, fasten to the same stitch, then complete the row, putting another trefoil at the end.

Work two rows of d c over the padding all round, fastening 7, 10, 10, 7 to the tip of the leaflets in the trefoil in the order named. Fasten off the padding, and a row of tr into each stitch, then a row of 2 tr separated by a ch, missing a tr beneath the ch, then 2 d c over the ch, 1 d c into each tr, with a 5 ch picot between the trs, the remaining rows of trs with picots is worked over a row of 10 ch loops. The motifs are joined in the picots at the end, the little space at the top filled in with a couple of bars worked over with double stitch, from a tiny ring of padding. Finish the top in the usual way with the straightening lines. With the straightening lines at both sides a lovely insertion can be made ; and without any lines, with the motifs merely joined, it forms a beautiful dress or lingerie trimming.

AN IRISH EDGING.

An Irish Edging.

A new design is shown here, very suitable for blouse trimming, and for adorning children's frocks and the finer kinds of lingerie. Use No. 80 Manlove's lace thread, with a short piece of stout linen thread for the centres, and a fine crochet hook. Fold a length of ten inches or so of the linen thread in two, insert the hook in the fold and make a double stitch, then 15 d c over the padding, pull the padding tight to make all the stitches as compact as possible, and twist round to form a circle, put the hook through the fourth d c, and form a double stitch over the padding, then continue working round and round for four rows, putting two stitches into each of preceding row.

Fasten off the padding neatly on the back, and cut away the superfluous thread. * 10 ch, 1 d c into the next third d c, 5 ch, 1 d c into same stitch as last, * and repeat all round. Slip stitch up to the top of the first loop, and * 10 ch, 1 d c into next loop, 5 ch, 1 d c into same loop, * and repeat for four rows. Slip stitch to top of next loop, and put 10 ch into each loop all round. Into each 10 ch space put * 10 d c, 6 ch, 1 d c, 12 ch into the d c between the loops, 6 ch into next sp, * then repeat all round. The motifs are connected at each side in four of the long picots at the centre of the 12 ch.

For the little circular figure in the spaces make 8 ch, form into a ring, into which put 12 d c, * 8 ch, picot 6 of them, 2 ch, join to the long picot in the next to the centre joining, 8 ch, picot 6 of them, 2 ch, 1 d c into next on ring, 2 d c into next two on ring, * and repeat, putting the second into the joining between the motifs, and the third into next long picot on next motif, and leaving the last free.

Make the straightening line at the top of 10 ch into each long picot, and into the circular figure, then over the ch stitches work a row of d c, putting 14 into each sp, next a row of trs separated by 4 ch over the four intervening d c; finish with a row of 6 d c into each sp.

For an insertion repeat this straightening at the other side. For the lace edging work the row of 10 ch into each long picot and into the joinings, then over this put * 21 d c, 10 ch, turn back and fasten to the fourteenth d c, 10 ch into seventh d c, 10 ch into first d c, turn and put 5 d c, 6 ch, 10 d c into first loop, 6 ch, 15 d c into next loop, 6 ch, 5 d c into next loop, 10 ch, turn back and fasten to the centre of middle loop, 10 ch into first loop between the picots, turn and put 5 d c, 6 ch, 10 d c into next loop, 6 ch, 5 d c into next loop, 10 ch, turn back and fasten to the last loop between the picots, turn, into top loop put 9 d c, 6 ch, 9 d c, 5 d c, 6 ch, 5 d c into next, the same into next, and repeat from *.

A Handsome Deep Lace.

Many connoisseurs in lace aver that some of the designs in the "old style" Irish crochet have never been equalled, and much prefer copies of these designs to the lace of the present day.

This deep lace is one of the designs referred to. It is worked in Manlove's No. 40 Irish lace thread, and there are only two designs in the motifs, which are so arranged as to give the appearance of variety. Commence the motif at the top left-hand corner by winding a coarse cotton thread (about No. 10) around a small mesh, such as a coarse steel knitting needle, 15 times, over this padded ring work d c as closely as possible with the No. 40 and a No. 7 crochet hook, 1 single into the first d c on the ring, 15 ch, turn these to the right and fasten to the ring, spacing the stitch so that the ring will accommodate nine more with equal spaces between.

* Turn, and over the end of the ch put 5 d c, 6 ch, 5 d c, 10 ch, fasten to the ring as in the preceding, and repeat from * nine times, taking up the last and first ch in the final d c's over the bar. 7 d c into each ch sp all round. In the next row, put * 3 d c into first three, 6 ch, 3 d c into next three, 10 ch, turn these back and fasten to the first d c, into this loop, 1 d c, 18 tr, 1 d c. Repeat from * over each sp.

For the second motif commence on the same kind of padded ring worked over in d c.

2nd Row.—1 d c into each on ring.

3rd Row.—18 tr into last row with 3 ch between.

4th Row.—* 5 tr into each of next

three sp, turn, 1 d c into first tr, 1 ch, 1 d c into every second tr, turn, 2 d c into each ch sp, turn, 2 ch, 1 d c over each d c in second last row, turn, 3 d c into each sp, 1 d c into end of last d c row, 3 ch into the sp between the tr. Repeat from * into every three sp.

Work two rows of "filling" around each motif, consisting of a number of equally spaced loops, each loop made thus: 8 ch, picot six of them, 5 ch, fasten to the edge with 1 d c. Connect the motifs in the loops at the sides by bars and picots, this will leave a small opening in the centre of each four motifs, fill in with a ring made exactly like the centre of the motif and connected to the loops all round with similar loops and picots.

Fill in the spaces at the top with a few picot loops, then make a "straightening line " of 5 ch, 1 tr into each loop, and finish the top with a row of 5 d c into each sp.

Around the scallops at the lower end make the "straightening line " of 3 ch, 1 tr at each side of a picot, putting 1 d c into the centre between two motifs instead of the tr.

For the edging, * 15 d c over the "straightening line," turn, 3 ch, 1 d c into the 10th, 5th, and 1st d c, turn, over the last d c put 1 d c, 6 ch, 1 d c, 3 ch, 1 d c into the centre sp, 3 ch, 1 d c into first sp, turn, slip stitch to centre of last loop, 3 ch, 1 d c into next loop, slip stitch down to next d c, turn, and put 2 d c, 6 ch, 2 d c into each sp down to the line, then repeat from *.

A HANDSOME DEEP LACE.

A Berry Design in Irish Bébé Insertion.

For this beautiful insertion use Manlove's No. 60 Irish lace thread with a No. 6 crochet hook. Commence at the three berries in the centre of each motif, by winding coarse cotton thread 15 times around a small mesh,

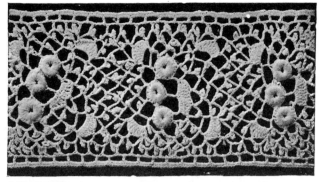

A BERRY DESIGN.

about one-sixteenth of an inch in diameter ; a coarse knitting needle will do, or anything of a similar size. Into this ring work double stitch as closely as possible, keeping all ends of thread at the side towards you, as the other side is the right side of the berry.

Join first and last stitches, make another padded ring, put the needle through the centre and work half-way round in double stitch as closely as possible, make another padded ring and take on the needle as before, work double stitch all round, join first and last stitches and make 1 d c over the stitch between this and the next ring, finish the other half of centre ring, join first and last stitches.

Break off the thread and fasten with 1 tr into the centre of lower half of end berry, 3 ch, 1 tr into centre of lower half of second berry, 3 ch, 1 tr into centre of next berry, turn and work 5 d c into each 3 ch sp, turn, work 1 tr into each d c, 1 d c over first d c, 8 ch, picot 5, 3 ch, 1 d c into next third on berry, * 8 ch, picot 5, 5 ch, 1 d c, * after last picot turning backwards; this is the picot loop of

which there are four, equally spaced, over the trs, and one into the fourth d c on next berry, turn and put a picot loop into each preceding loop, one over each of the berries, and one between them.

Put the last loop of this row after the first picot of the first loop in it. One picot loop into next loop, * 8 ch, fasten before the picot on next loop, turn, work 8 d c over the 8 ch, turn, 1 tr into each d c, 1 d c over first d c, 1 picot loop into same loop after the picot, 1 loop into each of next two, and repeat the group of trs followed by 3 picot loops, three times. Work a final row of picot loops, putting one into each of preceding row, 1 before, into the centre of, and at the end of the group of trs.

When a sufficient number of motifs are worked join up the sides with a row of picot loops divided between the loops at opposite sides. Work a "straightening" line of 1 tr, 3 ch alternately, putting the tr into each loop and after each picot along the edge, into this row put another of the same, and finish with 5 d c into each 3 ch sp.

Irish Crochet.

Bébé Crochet Lace set into the Material.

Irish bébé crochet has lost none of its popularity and is still largely used, the rose and shamrock being still the most popular. It is often used set into the material as shown here. The square motifs are made in the usual way, so that detailed directions are scarcely necessary. Use only fine thread for this lace; No. 60 Irish lace thread should be the coarsest used, but No. 80 makes a nicer lace, if somewhat more tedious in the working.

The motifs are connected with two of the picot loops into corresponding "groups of tr" at each side of the motifs, then the straightening lines are worked at both sides, the top portion finished with a row of d c, and the lower with a loop and picot. The edge of the material is cut to fit the lace and then worked over in button-hole stitch, to which the lace is neatly sewn on the back. This is a favourite way for trimming lingerie gowns, linen collars, cuffs, and lawn fichus, which give such a pretty, dressy look for this purpose, nothing could be more daintily suitable than this charming design worked with the finest thread.

BÉBÉ CROCHET LACE SET INTO THE MATERIAL.

Section V.

CROCHET USED WITH VARIOUS BRAIDS

A ROSE AND SHELL DESIGN.

I want to draw the attention of the needle-worker to the possibilities of crochet combined with Cash's Insertion Braids. For the decoration of household linen this work has the great virtue of wearing well. The braids strengthen the whole work in a wonderful manner, and add to its beauty at the same time. The designs on the next few pages would be suitable for tea-cloths, sideboard cloths, and suchlike articles; several of the designs also look exceedingly well when applied to blouses and washing dresses.

The Rose and Shell Design.

Prepare a piece of stiff paper with the lines marked upon it for the pattern, tack the braid and hemstitched linen in place, keeping the wrong side uppermost. Next sew the braid where it crosses, and at the points, with very neat small stitches. With Manlove's No. 80 Irish lace thread and a No. 7 crochet hook, work the picot filling in the triangles at top and bottom, putting one group of trs in the centre of each, and using the single picot filling.

For the tiny rose centre take a piece of coarse cotton, fold in two, insert the needle in the fold and work 15 double stitches over this padding, twist round to form a ring and fasten through the first stitch with a single stitch, then form five petals around the ring, each consisting of 1 d c, 7 tr, 1 d c over the padding and fastened to each third d c on ring, behind this work a second row of 10 tr in each petal, and each fastened to the stitch on the back between the petals in the first row. Work a third row of 12 tr in each, and fasten in the same way. Around this rose form 12 double picot loops fastening the twelfth into the first. Make a second row, and put a group of trs into each third loop of first, then do the " straightening

49

DOUBLE VANDYKE INSERTION.

**The
Shamrock
and
Triangle
Insertion.**

Arrange the braid as already directed, and for the shamrock take a few inches of coarse thread, fold in two, insert the hook at the folded end and form a d c with the fine crochet cotton, 45 d c over this padding, twist the last ten round to form a ring and fasten with a single stitch. Cross over the stem with 1 d c and form 3 loops of 6 ch each around the ring, cross over again and into each loop put 1 d c, 12 tr, 1 d c. Fasten off securely on the back and cut away the padding left over. Tack the shamrocks in place and connect all with the single picot loop, then finish off as

line " of trs divided by 4 ch, finish with a row of double stitches into each space as closely as possible. Tack one in the square space, face downwards, then top sew neatly to the braid all round.

Before removing the trimming from the pattern, press with a hot iron, then remove the tacking threads and place between folds of damped calico and press on the wrong side, take away the calico and finish off on the insertion itself to complete it.

SHAMROCKS AND TRIANGLES.

before. The illustration will show how to place them.

Double Vandyke Insertion.

This insertion is so simple that a glance at the illustration will enable anyone to copy it easily. Choose a narrow feather-stitched braid, and use very fine crochet cotton.

The Daisy Insertion.

Tack the braid on a piece of stiff paper on which the

DAISY INSERTION.

pattern has been marked. Sew the braid neatly where it crosses and to the top and lower part of the material, keeping the wrong side uppermost. For the daisy, wind thread round a small mesh to make the padded centre, into which work double stitch as closely as possible, 1 single through the first d c to close the ring, 10 loops of 6 ch each are placed around the ring evenly, into each loop work 1 d c, 6 tr, 1 d c. One daisy is put in the centre of each diamond, and half a daisy in each triangle.

Commence the half daisy in the

same way as the other, but put only 5 loops around it. Tack these in place after the manner illustrated, and connect with the braid by single picot bars.

Before removing the insertion from the pattern, press it with a hot iron, having previously placed a piece of damped calico over it.

Diagonal Shamrock Insertion.

The shamrocks in this pattern are made on a folded thread of rather coarse cotton ; insert the hook in the end, and with Manlove's No. 60 Irish lace thread make, over this padding throughout, 3 d c, 15 tr, 3 d c, pull the end of the padding to make the stitches as close as possible, 1 d c into the first d c to form into a ring. Repeat this twice more, then work a row of d c into each stitch all round the three leaflets, work 21 d c over the padding, turn, miss 2, and work a second row into the first. Fasten off on

DIAGONAL SHAMROCK INSERTION. 51

SHAMROCK EDGING.

20 d c over padding. These are sewn in place in the usual way and surrounded with a single picot filling. The edging consists of 6 ch loops into which 10 tr are worked, and then a row of 6 ch picots put between the tr. Finish the top portion in the usual way.

A Daisy Pattern.

The Daisy pattern is worked into a vandyke of the braid, which is surrounded by a picot edging. For the daisy, fold a strand of coarse cotton in two and form a tiny ring centre in the usual way; then around this work ten petals of two rows of double stitches over the padding, each row consisting of 22 stitches. Tack in the centre of the vandyke and connect it with a bar of picot filling. Work two rows of 10 ch loops at the top, and a third of 9 ch into each; over this last row work 10 d c into each space; the picot edging is worked into the braid

the back securely. Make a row of double picot loops all round, and a second row at each end with a group of trs at opposite corners; this forms the diamond shape motif, of which there are two in each space. Connect the motifs with a row of the filling, and work a straightened row all round of trs, alternating with 4 ch, spacing the trs so that the ch stitches form straight lines. Sew the strips of crochet neatly to the braid on the back of the work, then the insertion is ready to be worked into place on the material.

Shamrock Edging.

In the Shamrock design, the trefoil in the top row consists of three leaflets of 3 d c, 15 tr, 3 d c, over a double padding cord. The larger shamrock has two rows of 5 d c, 20 tr, 5 d c in each petal, and a stem of two rows of

A DAISY PATTERN.

on 7 ch loops worked over with double stitch and picots.

A Rose Design.

The Rose pattern has a row of tiny roses interspersed with baby filling between the rows of the braid, and a larger rose in the vandyke. This lace is finished with the picot loop around the vandyke and the usual straightening line at the top.

A ROSE PATTERN.

A DESIGN USING ONLY THE SIMPLEST STITCHES.

The Simplest of Edgings.

The remaining design shows some simple stitches used with a new braid Messrs. Cash & Co. have just brought out. It is very light-looking, resembling drawn-thread work.

It must be noted that several patterns of braid have been used in these edgings to show the designs. But in actual working keep to one pattern throughout each design.

A Broad Insertion in Vandyke Braid and Crochet.

Vandyke braid lends itself readily to use with crochet, as the following illustrations show.

Cut off sixteen points of braid and sew in a ring. Make a ring of 6 ch, 10 ch, 1 d c in point of braid just before the join, slip-stitch down 3 ch, 3 ch, 1 d c into next point of braid, slipstitch down 3 ch, 1 d c, 5 tr, 1 d c down the 10 ch, 1 d c in ring. Repeat all round. Make number of circles necessary for length required.

Sew six points of braid together, draw together the points in the centre to form a star to go between circles, † 1 d c into point of circle, 2 ch, 1 picot of 5 ch, 2 ch, 1 d c into point of small star, 2 ch, 1 picot, 2 ch, 1 d c into next point of circle, * 2 ch, 1 picot, 9 ch, 1 picot, 2 ch, 1 d c into next point, repeat from * three times; 2 ch, 1 picot, 2 ch, 1 d c into point of next star, 2 ch, 1 picot, 2 ch, 1 d c into point of circle, * 2 ch, 1 picot, 5 ch, 1 picot, 2 ch, 1 d c into next point, repeat from * once, 2 ch, 1 picot, 2 ch, repeat from †. Repeat work round all circles. To join—instead of working 2 ch, 1 picot,

53

With Various Braids.

5 ch, 1 picot, 2 ch, 1 d c—work 2 ch, 1 picot, 2 ch, catch third ch of last circle, 2 ch, 1 picot, 2 ch, 1 d c.

Edging.

1st Row.—1 d c into next point of star, 2 ch, * 5 d c on middle 5 ch of 9 ch between picots of last row, 2 ch, 1 picot, 9 ch, 1 picot, 2 ch ; repeat from * three times ; 1 d c into next point of star, 2 ch, 1 picot, 9 ch, 1 picot, 2 ch, turn, 5 d c between picots as before, 2 ch, 1 picot, 9 ch, 1 picot, 2 ch, 5 d c between next 2 picots, 2 ch, 1 picot, 9 ch, 1 picot, 5 d c as before, 2 ch, 1 picot, 9 ch, 1 picot, 2 ch, 1 d c into star. Repeat between each star on both sides.

2nd Row —* 1 d c into first point of star, 2 ch, 1 picot, 2 ch, 1 picot, 2 ch, 1 d c into next point of star, 2 ch, 1 picot, 2 ch, 1 d tr under first 9 ch of last row, 2 ch, 1 picot, 2 ch, 1 picot, 2 ch, 5 d c between last two picots, 2 ch, 1 picot, 2 ch, 1 picot, 2 ch, 5 d c as before, 2 ch, 1 picot, 2 ch, 1 picot, 2 ch, 1 d tr, 2 ch, 1 picot, 2 ch. Repeat from * on both sides.

3rd Row.—1 tr, 1 ch, miss 1. Repeat on both sides.

Block Insertion.

Cut off the length of twenty points of braid and sew neatly in a circle.

Make a ring of 5 ch, 1 d c into ring, 12 ch, catch point of braid before joining with 1 d c, slipstitch down 4 ch, 5 ch, catch next two points with 1 d c, slipstitch down the 5 ch, 4 ch, catch next point with 1 d c, slipstitch down the 4 ch, 3 d c, 1 picot of 4 ch, 10 d c down the remaining ch, 1 d c into ring, 10 ch, catch up next point with 1 d c, 3 d c, 1 picot of 4 ch, 10 d c down the 10 ch, 1 d c into ring. Repeat from beginning.

Make number of diamonds for length required and sew together (drawing into shape) by one point to make the joining squares.

For the Edges.

1st Row.—1 d c into second point from centre, 7 ch, 7 rows of d c on the 7 ch to form a square, 1 quadruple tr (thread four times over needle) in next point, 7 ch, join into next point, make another square as before, but at end of 6th row 1 d c into corresponding point of next braid diamond, another row of d c to finish square, 1 quadruple tr into next point, 7 ch, another square, at end of 6th row work d c into next point, another row of d c to finish square. Break off and repeat from beginning of row.

2nd Row.—* 1 d c into centre point, 10 ch, 1 triple tr into next point, 7 d c on square, 5 ch, thread 5 times over needle, 1 quadruple tr on top of quadruple tr of

A BROAD INSERTION.

previous row, thread four times over needle, work same tr on next quadruple tr, draw thread through remaining threads on needle, 5 ch, 7 d c on top of square, 1 triple tr on next point, 10 ch. Repeat from *.

3rd Row.—1 tr, 1 ch miss 1. Repeat.

4th Row.—Begin on wrong side of work, 1 d c, * 7 ch, miss 1 tr, 1 d c into next, turn work, 4 d c, 1 picot of 5 ch, 4 d c into the 7 ch, leaving 3 or 4 ch free. Repeat from *.

5th Row.—1 tr, 1 ch, miss 1. Repeat.

Work from 1st row on the other side of diamonds.

Block Edging to Match the Insertion.

BLOCK EDGING TO MATCH THE INSERTION.

BLOCK INSERTION.

* Join in point of braid, 7 ch, 7 rows of d c, to form a square, 1 d tr into next point, 7 ch, join to third point, and make another square. At end of 6th row of d c catch third point from needle (the two points passed over should be sewn together), at end of 7th row of d c make 1 d tr into next point, and then make another square of 7 rows of d c. Break off. Repeat from *, joining into fourth point of braid from last, worked into top edge.

1st Row.—* 1 d c into centre point, 10 ch, 1 triple tr into next point, 7 d c on square, 5 ch, thread over needle five times, 1 quadruple tr on d tr of previous row, thread four times over needle, 1 quadruple tr on next d tr, draw thread through the stitches left on needle, 5 ch, 7 d c on next square, 1 triple tr on next point, 10 ch. Repeat from *.

2nd Row.—1 tr, 1 ch, miss 1. Repeat.

3rd Row.—Begin on wrong side of work; 1 d c, * 7 ch, miss 1 tr, 1 d c into next, turn work, 4 d c, 1 picot of 5 ch, 4 d c into the 7 ch, leaving 3 or 4 ch free. Repeat from *.

4th Row.—1 tr, 1 ch, miss 1. Repeat.

Bottom Edge.

1st Row.—Begin side of work; 1 d c into first point of braid (beginning

55

With Various Braids.

left side of work\, * 7 ch, 1 d c into next point of braid, turn work, 4 d c, 1 picot of 5 ch, 4 d c into 7 ch, repeat from * three times, 8 ch, 1 d c into middle point, 4 d c, 1 picot, 4 d c, 10 ch, 1 d c into same point, 8 ch, 1 d c into next point, 4 d c, 1 picot, 4 d c into the 8 ch, * 7 ch, 1 d c into next point, 4 d c, 1 picot, 4 d c into 7 ch, repeat from * twice, 5 ch, catch two centre points together, 4 d c, 1 picot, 4 d c into 5 ch, 5 ch, 1 d c into next point, 4 d c, 1 picot, 4 d c into 5 ch. Repeat from beginning of row.

2nd Row.—3 d c, 1 picot of 5 ch, 2 d c, 1 picot, 3 d c. Repeat, except in centre loops, where work 2 d c, 1 picot, repeat four times, 2 d c.

A Handsome Edge for Blinds or Valances.

Sew together fourteen points of braid to form a star. Add a little ring made of d c over ch. Join in one point of star with 1 d c, 5 ch, 1 picot of 5 ch, 3 ch, take up another piece of braid and work 1 tr into point, 4 ch, 1 picot, 3 ch, 1 d c into next point of star, * 4 ch, 1 picot, 3 ch, 1 tr into next point of braid, leave two stitches on needle, 1 tr into next point, draw thread straight through last three stitches, 4 ch, 1 picot, 3 ch, join into next point of star. Repeat from * five times, 3 ch, 1 picot, 4 ch, 1 tr into braid, 3 ch, 1 picot, 5 ch, 1 d c into point of star. Break off, leaving five points of star free. Repeat from beginning for length required, leaving one point of braid between each star.

Top Edge.

1st Row.—1 d tr into 5 ch between star and picot, 5 ch, 1 d tr into point of star, 5 ch, 1 tr into next point of star, 5 ch, 1 d c into next point, 5 ch, 1 tr into point, 5 ch, 1 d tr, 5 ch, 1 d tr into 5 ch between star and picot, ch, cotton over needle six times, work into space between next point of braid, 11 ch, 1 picot of 5 ch, 1 ch, 1 d c into middle point

A HANDSOME EDGE FOR BLINDS OR VALANCES.

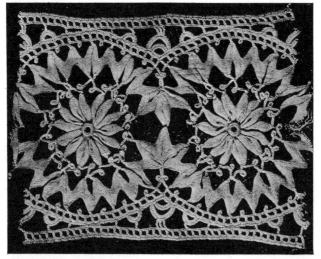

INSERTION TO MATCH THE VALANCE EDGING.

of braid, 1 ch, 1 picot of 5ch, 2 ch, catch into ninth ch of 11 ch just worked, 9 ch, cotton over needle six times as before. Repeat from beginning of row.

2nd Row.—1 tr, 2 ch, miss 2. Repeat.

3rd Row.—Work over chain with d c.

Bottom Edge.

1st Row.—1 d c into point of braid, 10 ch, join into fourth to make a picot, 3 ch, join into next point. Repeat nine times, 10 ch, 1 picot, 3 ch, join four points of braid together with 1 d c, 10 ch, 1 picot, catch picots together, 3 ch, 1 d c into next point of braid. Repeat from beginning of row.

2nd Row.—1 tr, 2 ch, miss 2. Repeat.

3rd Row.—2 d c into each of the first two spaces made by tr and ch of last row, 1 picot of 4 ch, 8 d c, turn, 1 d c into third d c of those just worked, turn and fill 8 ch with d c, * 6 d c, 8 ch, turn, 1 d c into third d c, turn, fill ch with d c, 1 d c, 12 ch, turn, 1 d c into fourth d c, turn, fill 12 ch with d c. Repeat from * four times, There will be 2 d c between each 6 d c, 8 ch, turn, 1 d c into fourth d c, turn, fill 8 ch with d c, 1 picot, 4 d c. Repeat from beginning, joining the picots together.

Insertion to Match the Valance Edging.

The insertion is made the same way as the lace, by sewing together fourteen points of braid to form a star, 1 d c into point of star, 4 ch, picot of 5 ch, 3 ch, take up another piece of braid and work 1 tr into point, 4 ch, 1 picot, 3 ch, 1 d c into next point of star, 4 ch, 1 picot, 3 ch, 1 d c into point of braid, 4 ch, 1 picot, 3 ch, 1 d c into star, * 4 ch, 1 picot, 3 ch,

1 tr leaving last two stitches on needle, 1 tr into next point, draw thread straight through last three stitches, 4 ch, 1 picot, 3 ch, 1 d c into star. Repeat from * twice. 4 ch, 1 picot, 3 ch, 1 tr into point of braid, 4 ch, 1 picot, 3 ch, 1 d c into star, 4 ch, 1 picot, 3 ch, 1 tr into braid, 4 ch, 1 picot, 3 ch, 1 d c into star. Repeat round other half of star, taking up another piece of braid. Work number of stars required for length, leaving one point of braid between each star.

Top and Bottom Edges.

1st Row.—* 1 tr into point of braid, 10 ch, join into fourth to make a picot, 3 ch, 1 tr into point. Repeat from * six times, 10 ch, 1 picot, 4 ch, catch together four points of braid with 1 d c, 11 ch, join into fifth to form a picot, 1 d c into corresponding picot, 3 ch. Repeat from beginning.

2nd Row.—1 tr, 2 ch, miss 2. Repeat, but work no ch over the four points joined together.

3rd Row.—10 d c, 8 ch, turn 1 d c into eighth d c from beginning, turn, work d c into ch, * 22 d c, 8 ch, turn, 1 d c into twentieth d c from last loop, turn, fill 8 ch with d c, 10 d c, 8 ch, turn, 1 d c into sixth d c from last loop, fill 8 ch with d c, 2 d c, 12 ch, turn, 1 d c into fifth d c from same loop as before, fill 12 ch with d c, 6 d c, 8 ch, turn, 1 d c into third d c, fill 8 ch with d c. Repeat from *.

4th Row.—1 tr on top of first loop, 8 ch, miss 4 d c, 1 tr, 8 ch, miss 4 d c, 4 d c on next 4 d c, 8 ch, miss 4 d c, 1 tr, 8 ch, 1 tr on top of loop, 8 ch, 3 d tr on top of large loop, 8 ch. Repeat from beginning.

5th Row.—1 tr, 2 ch, miss 2. Repeat.

6th Row.—Work over ch with d c.

57

With Various Braids.

MARGUERITE EDGING.

Marguerite Edging.

8 ch, join to form a ring.

1st Row.—16 d c to fill ring.

2nd Row.—3 ch, miss 1, 1 d c in next stitch. Repeat 7 times.

3rd Row.—3 ch, 2 tr all caught in one into first 3 ch of last row (leave last thread on needle each time, thread over needle, draw through all and finish with 1 s c), * 5 ch, 3 tr caught in one into next 3 ch. Repeat from * 6 times, 5 ch.

4th Row.—* 4 d c, 3 ch to form picot, 2 d c, 1 picot, 2 d c, 1 picot, 4 d c into 5 ch of last row, repeat from * once; 4 d c into next 5 ch, 1 picot, 2 d c, 1 picot, 2 d c, 2 ch, catch point of braid, 2 ch, 4 d c, 4 d c into next 5 ch, 2 ch, catch next point, 2 ch, 2 d c, 1 picot, 2 d c, 2 ch, catch next point, 2 ch, 4 d c, 4 d c into next 5 ch, 2 ch, catch next point, 2 ch, 2 d c, 2 ch, catch next point, 2 ch, 2 d c, 2 ch, catch next point, 2 ch, 4 d c, 4 d c under next 5 ch, 2 ch, catch up next point, 2 ch, 2 d c, 1 picot, 2 d c, 2 ch, catch next point, 2 ch, 4 d c, 4 d c, into next 5 ch, 2 ch, catch next point, 2 ch, 2 d c, 1 picot, 2 d c, 1 picot, 4 d c, 4 d c into next 5 ch, 1 picot, 2 d c, 1 picot, 2 d c, 1 picot, 4 d c, break off.

Repeat from first row, pass two points of braid and join in third.

Straight Edge.

1st Row.—1 d c in first point, thread twice over needle, 1 tr in next point, draw through twice only, 1 tr into last 3 picots of round in centre and work off all stitches, 2 d tr caught in one, where trs join, * 5 ch, 1 tr into middle of next 3 picots, 4 ch, then 1 d c, 1 ch into each of the next 3 picots, 4 ch, 1 tr in centre of next picots, 5 ch, thread twice over needle, 1 tr into first of next group of picots, 1 tr in point of braid, 2 d tr caught in one, where last 2 tr join 5 ch, thread twice over needle, 1 tr in same point of braid, 1 tr in next point of braid, 2 d tr on top as before, 5 ch, thread twice over needle, 1 tr in same point of braid, 1 tr in second unattached picot, 2 d tr on top caught together. Repeat from *.

2nd Row.—1 tr, 1 ch, miss 1. Repeat.

Edge below Braid.

1st Row.—1 d c in first point of braid, * 2 ch, thread twice over needle, 1 tr on side of point of braid, 1 tr on opposite side, work off all stitches, 3 ch, 1 tr where the two others cross, 2 ch, 1 d c in next picot, repeat from * six times, 4 ch, catch next 3 points of braid with 1 d c, 4 ch, 1 d c in next point. Repeat from beginning of row.

2nd Row.—* 2 d c into 2 ch of last row, 2 d c, 3 picots of 3 ch each separated by 2 d c, 2 d c under 3 ch of last row, 2 d c into next hole of 2 ch. Repeat from * six times, 2 d c into 4 ch of last row, 2 d c into next 4 ch. Repeat from beginning of row.

A Good Wearing Edging.

Make a ring of 7 ch, 3 ch, 1 tr into the ring. Count off sixteen points of braid and lay the sixteenth over the second point and catch the two together with 1 d c; this makes a large circle of braid ; 1 ch, 2 tr, caught together in ring of chain, 1 ch, catch two following points together (one on top of the other as before), 1 ch, 2 tr as before in ring, 1 ch, catch the following two points together, 1 ch, 2 tr in ring, 1 ch and continue as before all round, but working into circle of braid only, that is so say, the braid has been caught double three times and the other points singly. Break off.

Count off six points from last one worked, mark with needle and thread, count fifteen points from this, sew the sixth and fifteenth together to make a circle ; this will keep them in place while making the centre ring, which is worked like the first.

Edge Round Scallop.

1st Row.—1 d c, catching together first point of braid and first point of circle, 4 ch, 1 d c into next point. Repeat. 3 ch is sufficient between the three straight points between circles.

2nd Row.—Into first 4 ch of last row, 2 d tr caught together, * 2 d tr into next 4 ch. 1 picot of 4 ch, 2 d tr, 1 picot, 2 d tr. Repeat from * six times, 2 d tr into next 4 ch, 2 d tr into each following loop of ch, leaving one stitch on needle after every d tr, draw

thread through all nine stitches, 2 d tr into next 4 ch, 2 d tr into next 4 ch, 1 ch, catch opposite picot, 1 ch, 2 d tr, 1 ch, catch opposite picot, 1 ch, 2 d tr. Repeat from beginning of row.

Top Edge.

1st Row.—1 tr, 4 ch into each point ; this must be kept very straight, and care must be taken to catch the double points as if they were one. Repeat.

2nd Row.—1 d c on top of tr, * 4 ch, 2 d tr caught together on same tr, 3 ch, 1 d c on top of next tr, 5 ch, 1 d c on next tr. Repeat from *.

3rd Row.—4 ch, 1 d c into tr of last row, 4 ch, 1 d c into centre of 5 ch. Repeat.

4th Row.—1 tr, 1 ch, miss 1. Repeat.

Ivy Leaf Insertion.

1st Row.—* 1 d c into point of braid, 4 ch, 2 d tr caught into 1 (leave last thread on needle each time, thread over needle, draw through all three at once, and finish with 1 s c) into d c, 4 ch, 2 d tr caught in one, on top of last d tr, 1 d c into next of braid ; repeat from * for length required.

2nd Row.—Same as 1st Row on other side of braid.

3rd Row.—* tr between first two groups of d tr, 4 ch, 1 tr on point of braid, 4 ch, 1 tr between the d tr, 4 ch, cotton three times over needle, insert

A GOOD WEARING EDGING.

With Various Braids.

needle in point of braid, and work off in twos until three are left on needle, cotton over needle, needle into next point of braid, work off in twos. Repeat from *.

4th Row.—Same as 3rd Row on other side of braid.

5th Row.—1 tr, 1 ch, miss 1. Repeat to end of row.

6th Row.—Same as 5th Row, on other side.

IVY LEAF INSERTION.

Chestnut Leaf Edging.

Edging Above Braid.

1st Row.—8 ch, catch point of braid with 1 tr, 10 ch, * fasten 2 points with 3 triple tr caught in one (leave last thread on needle each time, thread over needle, draw through all, and finish with 1 s c) ; repeat from * four times ; 10 ch, 1 tr into next point of braid, 7 ch, 1 d c into next point. Repeat from beginning for length required.

2nd Row.—* 1 d c into each chain and first tr stitches, thread twice over needle, fasten into top of first triple tr, draw through once, thread over needle, catch up last triple tr, and work off in the usual way, 7 ch. Repeat from *.

3rd Row.—1 tr, 1 ch, miss 1. Repeat to end of row.

4th Row.—* 1 cross tr (cotton over needle twice, insert needle into tr, work off until 3 threads are left on needle, thread over needle, insert needle into next tr, and work off as usual, 1 ch, 1 tr where the two join), 1 ch. Repeat from *.

5th Row.—1 tr, 1 ch, miss 1, repeat.

Edging Below Braid.

1 d c into first point of braid, 6 ch, 1 d c into next point, * 3 ch, 6 tr each separated by a picot of 4 ch into next point, 3 ch, 1 d c into next point, repeat from * twice, 3 ch, 1 d c into next two points taken together, 3 ch, 1 d c into next point, 3 ch, 1 d c into next two points, 3 ch, 1 d c in next point, 3 ch, turn work, catch in opposite point, turn work, 3 ch, slipstitch into last point, 4 ch, 1 d c in next point. Repeat from *.

Broad Star Lace.

Join 16 points of braid in a circle ; sew points in centre together.

CHESTNUT LEAF EDGING.

1 d c into first point, * 2 ch, 1 picot of 5 ch, 3 ch, 1 picot, 2 ch, 1 d c into next point. Repeat from * all round.

Work each circle in the same way, catching them together twice between the picots.

Work 2 rows of large circles.

The Small Circles.

Make circle of 12 points of braid, 1 d c into 1st point, * 1 ch, 1 picot, 2 ch, join to large circle in second sp from where it is joined to the other large circle, 2 ch, 1 picot, 1 ch, 1 d c into next point. Repeat from * once, 6 ch, 1 tr just where large circles are

The Small Circles at Top of Lace.

1 d c into point, 1 ch, 1 picot, 2 ch, join to large circles as before, 2 ch, 1 picot, 1 ch, 1 d c into next point of small circle. Repeat once, 6 ch, 1 tr where large circles are joined, 2 ch, 1 picot, 1 d c into third ch, 2 ch, 1 l c

BROAD STAR LACE.

joined, 2 ch, 1 picot, 1 d c into third ch from point, 2 ch, 1 d c into point of small circle. Repeat from beginning all round circle. Continue making these circles until required length is obtained.

into point, 1 ch, 1 picot, 2 ch, join to large circle, 2 ch, 1 picot, 1 ch, 1 d c into point of small circle, 1 ch, 1 picot, 2 ch, join to large circle, 2 ch, 1 picot, 2 ch, 1 d c into point, * 3 ch, 1 picot, 3 ch, 1 picot, 3 ch, 1 d c into next

space of large circle. Repeat from *
twice. Work the number of circles
required in the same way.

1 s c into first point worked into
the small circle, 3 ch, 1 d c into
next point, 2 ch, 1 picot, 2 ch, 1 picot,
1 d c between the two picots of previous
row. * 2 ch, 1 picot, 2 ch, 1 picot, 2
ch, 1 d c between two picots as before.
Repeat from * twice, but work last
d c into point of next small circle, 3
ch, 1 d c into point of braid to
correspond with the other end. Break

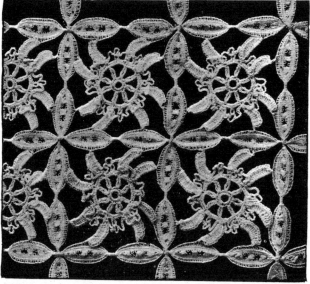

DESIGN NO. 1.

off and start again the other side of
circle. Continue to end of row.

1 tr into first free point of small
circle, 3 ch, 1 tr into next point, 3 ch,
1 tr into next point, 4 ch, 1 tr between
the two picots of previous row, 5 ch,
miss two picots, 1 tr between picots
as before, 5 ch, 1 tr as before, 5 ch, 1
tr, 4 ch. Repeat to end of row.

1 tr, 1 ch, miss 1 ch, 1 tr.

Bottom Edge.

1st Row.—1 d tr between picots, 2
ch, 1 picot, 1 d tr between next pair

of picots. Repeat to end of row, but
work 1 d c instead of 1 d tr between
circles.

2nd Row.—1 d c into each ch; after
the third d c after picot work 7 ch,
turn work, 1 d c into third d c the
other side of picot; turn and work
12 d c into the loop of 7 ch. Continue
as before. Between the circles work
the d c as far as the picot, 2 ch across
to next large circle.

**All-over Designs
with Honiton Braid.**

Design No. 1.

Select fine Honiton
braid with half-inch
lobes separated by bars
about an eighth of an
inch long. Use Man-
love's No. 60 crochet
thread. For whatever
purpose required the
best way is to place
the braid on the paper
pattern, crossing two
pieces at the bars be-
tween the second and
third lobes as illus-
trated, fasten the cross-
ings with a tight d c
at each side to keep
the braid in place and
preserve the square.

Each square is then filled in with
the motif, for which make 8 ch, and
form into a ring, 16 d c into the ring,
1 single through the first d c, 4 ch to
stand for a long tr, 1 long tr into first
d c, 5 ch, 2 long tr into every second
d c, into each space put 3 d c, 6 ch,
3 d c.

In the next row put * 10 ch into the
centre of one of the braid lobes, fasten
with a d c, turn, and over the 10 ch
put 1 d c, 12 tr, 1 d c, 1 d c into next
on ring, 8 ch. 1 d c into the picot

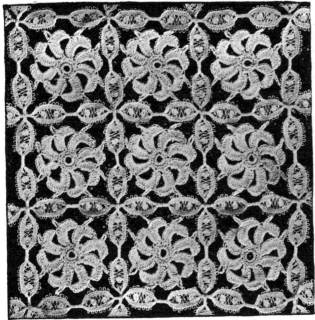

DESIGN NO. 2.

All-over Laces with Honiton Braid.

into next 2 on ring, 10 ch, fasten to the stitch after the picot in preceding leaflet with a d c, then over the ch put 1 d c, 5 tr, 3 ch, 1 d c into centre picot on next lobe of braid, 3 ch, 5 tr over the 10 ch, putting the needle through the last tr as before, 1 d c into same stitch on the ring as the last d c, and repeat from * six times. Fasten off the thread neatly on the back.

Design No. 3.

The lobes in this braid are nearly cir-

twice, 8 ch, 1 d c over next tr, and repeat from * all round. Fasten off neatly on the back.

Design No. 2.

Cross the braid as in the preceding design, and secure with a tight d c at both sides. For the motif, form 8 ch into a ring, into which put 16 d c, 1 single through the first d c on the ring, 10 ch, 1 d c through the stitch next to the needle, 1 tr through next stitch, 4 tr over the ch stitches, 3 ch, 1 d c through a picot on the centre of a lobe in the braid, 3 ch, put the needle through the top of last tr, and form a tr over the ch stitches, 4 tr over the ch, 1 d c into the stitch on the ring close to the first of the 10 ch, * 2 d c

cular, and the squares are arranged in the same way as the preceding design. Use fine crochet cotton with a correspondingly fine crochet-hook. Form 8 ch into a ring, into which put 16 d c, 1 single through the first d c on the ring, 4 ch, 2 long tr into the first d c on ring, 5 ch, 3 long tr into

DESIGN NO. 3.

63

With Various Braids.

second next d c, 5 ch, 3 long tr into every second d c (8 groups of tr in all), 5 ch, 1 d c through the top of 1st group, 4 d c, 6 ch, 4 d c into first space,

FINE BRAID AND CROCHET LACE.

* 3 ch, 1 d c into the centre edge on a lobe of the braid, 3 ch, 4 d c, 6 ch, 4 d c into next space, and repeat from * all round. Fasten off securely on the back.

Fine Braid and Crochet Lace.

Fine braid having seven picots at each side of a loop was selected for this lace, which was worked with Barbour's No. 80 Linen Lace Thread. For the top portion fasten the thread with a d c to the first picot on a loop, * 10 ch, 1 d c into last picot on same loop, 5 ch, 3 long tr over next bar, 5 ch, 1 d c into next picot on next loop, repeat from * three times, 10 ch, 1 d c into last picot on loop, 10 ch, 3 long tr into three centre picots on next loop, 3 ch, 3 long tr into the three centre picots on next loop, repeat the 3 ch, 3 long tr until there are five groups of 3 tr, 1 d c through the top of first 3 tr, 10 ch, 1 d c into next picot on next loop, 10 ch, 1 d c into last picot on same loop, 1 d c into the corresponding d c on the fifth loop, 5 ch, 3 long tr over next bar, 5 ch, 1 d c into next picot, and repeat from the beginning.

In the next row put 10 d c into each 5 ch sp, and 20 d c into the 10 ch, on the 10 ch over the 4th loop put 10 d c and cross over to the corresponding 10 ch, and work 10 d c over the upper portion, then continue on.

For the straightening row fasten the thread to the centre of the 10 d c, after the second group of tr, with a tr, 8 ch, 1 tr into the centre of the 20 d c, 8 ch, 1 tr into centre of next loop, 8 ch, 1 triple tr into centre of next loop, 1 triple tr into corresponding loop on next section, 8 ch, and repeat from the beginning.

Finish this line with a row of d c into the spaces.

For the lower portion, work the 3 long tr into the 3 centre picots, with 3 ch between, on the first 5 loops, join first and last tr with 1 d c, 10 ch, * 3 long tr over next bar, 5 ch, 1 d c into next picot, 10 ch, 1 d c into last picot on same loop, 5 ch and repeat from * five times, ch 10, then repeat from the beginning.

In the next row work d c into each space as at the top portion, crossing over to the next section at the centre of the 10 ch, over the fifth braid loop in each mitre, then put a second row of d c into the first, putting a 6 ch picot after each fifth d c, forming a bar of 5 ch after the fourth loop to connect the mitres, and working the two rows of d c and picots over it.

Braid and Crochet Insertion.

Very fine Honiton braid was selected for this design with Barbour's No. 70 Linen Lace Thread.

Make a d c into the centre edge in a lobe in the braid, * 6 ch, put the hook through the first ch and form 2 long tr, retaining the last loop in each until the second is formed, then hooking the thread through all on the needle together, 6 ch and repeat the 2 long tr through the first of them, fasten with a d c to the centre of next lobe and repeat from * along one side of the braid.

2nd Row.—1 d c between the first two groups of tr, * 10 ch 1 d c into each of next 6 groups, 1 d c into each of next 6 groups, connect these 6 groups with a d c into the first of the 6 d c, and repeat from *.

3rd Row.—Fasten the thread through the centre of the second 10 ch with a d c, 10 ch, 1 d c into the d c between the tr and the next fifth ch, until 6 loops are formed, cross over to the second loop on next mitre with a d c, and repeat the 6 loops over each mitre.

4th Row.—* 3 long tr into first loop, 4 ch, 1 tr into next loop, 4 ch, 3 d c into each of next two loops, 4 ch, 1 tr into next loop, 4 ch, 3 long tr into next loop and repeat from * without any ch between the long tr groups.

5th Row.—5 d c into each space, crossing over the 3 d c with 3 ch.

6th Row.—4 ch 1 tr into every fifth stitch of last row.

7th Row.—4 d c into each space.

Repeat from the first at the opposite side of the braid.

A Narrow Lacy Edging.

Fine lace braid with Ardern's No. 40 crochet cotton.

Commence at the lower edge by putting in the

1st Row.—4 tr, 6 ch, 4 tr into first oval, 6 ch, 4 tr over the bar, 6 ch, into next oval 4 tr, 5 ch, 4 tr, 6 ch, 4 tr over the bar, 6 ch, into next oval 4 tr, 5 ch, 4 tr, into next oval 4 tr in the centre, then repeat from the beginning.

2nd Row.—2 d c over first 5 ch, * 6 ch, 2 d c over next 6 ch, 6 ch, 2 d c over next 6 ch, 6 ch into the space between the two groups of tr, on next oval put 4 tr, 5 ch, 2 long tr, 5 ch, 4 tr, 6 ch, 2 d c over next 6 ch, 6 ch, 2 d c over next 6 ch, 6 ch, 4 tr into the space between tr on next oval, miss the next oval and into the space between tr on the second put 4 tr, and repeat from *.

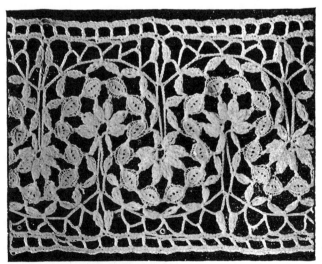

BRAID AND CROCHET INSERTION.

A NARROW LACY EDGING.

3rd Row.—5 d c into each ch space with 3 ch between, into the space between the tr put 3 ch, 7 tr, 5 ch, 7 tr, and repeat from the beginning.

4th Row.—7 ch, 2 d c into each space with 5 d c over the 5 ch between the tr.

5th Row.—* over first loop 3 d c, 5 ch, 3 d c over next 3 d c, 5 ch, 3 d c, 5 ch, 3 d c, repeat these two into next two loops, then over the 5 d c on the centre 8 ch, picot 5 of them, 3 ch, work down the side of the scallop to correspond. and repeat from *.

For the upper portion—

1st Row.—Into the first top centre oval put * 4 tr, 6 ch, 2 tr, 6 ch, 4 tr, 6 ch, 4 tr over the bar, 6 ch, 4 tr into the centre of each of next 3 ovals, 6 ch, 4 tr over the bar and repeat from * with 6 ch before.

2nd Row.—Into each of first 2 spaces 5 d c with 3 ch between, 7 ch, 2 long tr into next space. 9 ch, 2 long tr into next space between each group of 4 tr and the following space, 9 ch, 2 long tr into next space, 7 ch and repeat from the beginning.

3rd Row.—* 2 tr into first d c, 5 ch, 2 tr over the 3 ch, 5 ch, 2 tr into fifth d c, 9 ch, 9 d c into next space, 1 d c into each tr, 9 d c into next space, 9 ch and repeat from *

4th Row.—* 4 tr into first space, 3 ch, 4 tr into next, 3 ch, 4 long tr into next, 26 ch, 1 d c between the second and third groups of long tr, 26 ch, 4 long tr into next sp, 3 ch and repeat from *.

5th Row.—1 d c into each tr, 3 d c over each 3 ch, 9 d c over 26 ch, cross over to next 26 ch and put 9 d c over the last 9.

An Open Lacy Edging.

Fine lace braid with oval medallions separated by short bars.

Manlove's lace thread No. 42 and a fine crochet hook were employed in making this lace.

There are four rows at the top portion.

1st Row.—Into the spaces on edge of first oval of which there should be 10, 4 tr, 5 ch, 2 tr, 5 ch, 4 tr, having a tr in each space ; into the centre spaces on each of next three ovals put

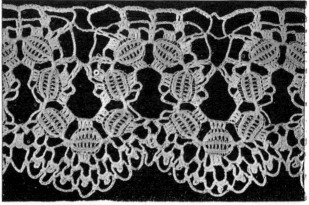

AN OPEN LACY EDGING.

4 tr, into next oval repeat the first, * 5 ch, 2 tr over next bar, 5 ch into next oval, 4 tr into first four spaces, 5 ch, 2 tr into next two spaces, 5 ch, 4 tr into next four spaces, and repeat from * twice, then repeat from 4 tr into centre four spaces of next 3 ovals and repeat from the beginning.

MARGUERITE DESIGN WITH RICE BRAID.

2nd Row.—2 tr over first 5 ch, * 2 tr into last 5 ch on fourth next oval, 2 tr into the 2 tr over the bar, 2 tr into the 5 ch before the 2 tr on centre of next oval, 6 ch, 4 tr over next 5 ch, 6 ch, 2 tr into next 2 tr, 6 ch, 4 tr into next 5 ch over the oval, 6 ch, 2 tr over next 5 ch, 8 ch, 2 tr into next 2 tr, 2 tr into first 5 ch on next oval and repeat from *.

3rd Row.—1 d c between the first 2 tr on the first oval at the top, 9 ch, * 2 tr into centre 2 of next 4 tr, 7 ch, 2 tr into next 2, 7 ch, 2 tr into centre of next 4, 16 ch, 1 d c into next 2 tr, 6 ch, cross over to opposite 2 tr, into which put 1 d c, 16 ch, then repeat from *.

4th Row.—Work d c into each space, 9 d c over the 16 ch, crossing over to the next 16 ch with 6 ch, and putting 9 d c over this also.

At the lower side there are 4 rows also.

1st Row.—4 tr into 4 centre spaces on first oval, 5 ch, 1 tr into next space, * 7 ch, 3 d c over the bar, 7 ch, into next oval 1 tr, 5 ch, 4 tr, 5 ch, 1 tr, then repeat from * three times, and after the 4 tr cross over to next oval and put 4 tr into it and following one, 5 ch, 1 tr into next space on same oval, repeat from the first 7 ch.

2nd Row.—3 d c over each ch space on the 3 centre ovals that form the scallop, 9 ch between, cross over to next 3 on next scallop, after putting 3 d c after 4 tr, and put 3 d c before the 4 tr, then repeat to the end.

3rd Row.—Over each ch space put 3 d c, 5 ch, 3 d c, then between put 7 ch, except where the scallops meet, where the 7 ch is omitted.

4th Row.—9 ch, 2 d c, into each ch space.

Marguerite Design with Rice Braid.

The pretty braid, known as Rice Braid, or Coronation Braid, lends itself to the formation of many beautiful designs, and is particularly good where loops are employed to form the petals for flowers. The peculiarity of this braid is that part of it is thick and part of it is thin.

Use Barbour's No. 40 Linen Lace Thread and a crochet hook of corresponding fineness. Fasten the thread to end of braid, work 15 d c over it as closely as possible, join first and last stitches with 1 d c, then working over the braid put 2 d c into each on centre. Fold the next two sections of the braid and put 2 d c into first two on centre over the thin part between the sections, thus forming a petal of two sections of the braid, repeat the petal until 15 are formed, then fasten off the braid on the back, and cut away the end. Into each d c around the centre where the petals are joined on, put a loop of 7 ch. Form a Clones knot[1] over the centre to fill in the sp. When a sufficient number of these Marguerites is done, work 3 rows of double picot filling all round, putting a group of trs after each 3rd loop in the 3rd row, then work 4 loops down the side and connect 2 motifs at opposite sides with one picot bar. Work 2 rows of straightening at the top of 5 ch, 1 tr, and finish with a row of 5 d c into each sp.

Work 1 row of the same straightening around the lower edge, and for the final edging * 18 d c over the straightening line, 8 ch, turn these to the right and fasten to the 11th d c, into this loop put 10 d c, 3 d c over the straightening line, turn, 3 ch, 1 tr into every 2nd d c on the loop, 3 ch, 1 d c into the 3rd d c beyond the loop, turn, put 1 d c, 4 tr, 1 d c into each sp, and repeat from *.

Sun-ray Design.

To begin this, 6 loops are formed on a centre ring of 9 ch worked over with d c, and connected with a d c in the 2nd row. Leave four sections of the braid between the loops and connect them by the crochet motif, which consists of a centre loop into which 10 tr are put, then the bars, and leaves formed on 10 ch, connect the points

all round with 12 ch, over which work the d c and little picot loops. To complete the pattern, finish the top part with 2 rows of straightening.

Flower-star Design.

For the centre of star make 6 ch, form into a ring, 3 ch, 18 tr into the ring, 1 s c through the 3rd ch, 1 d c into next tr, 10 ch, 1 d c into same tr, up the right side work into the loop 3 d c, 6 tr, take a piece of braid and join at the thin portion with 1 d c, 6 tr, 3 d c into the loop, 1 d c into next tr on ring, 5 ch, 1 d c into next tr, 1 d c into next tr, then repeat this until six petals are formed, joining the braid at each next thin section for three petals at one side, and taking another piece for the following three. Connect the motifs at each 3rd petal, keeping one piece of the braid at each side. The bars at the outside of the centre motifs are ch stitches covered with d c having a

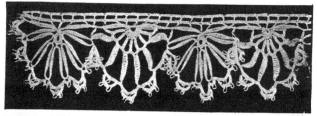

SUN-RAY DESIGN.

FLOWER-STAR DESIGN.

[1]See page 113.

picot in the centre. Finish with the usual straightening line at the top. At the lower edge, 16 ch loops are worked over with 5 d c in forming the first row, then 1 d c, 7 tr, 1 d c into each sp in

DOUBLE RING DESIGN.

the 2nd row, putting 10 d c into each of the two centre loops.

Double Ring Design.

Twist the cord into two rings, over-lapping each other, allowing one thick section of the cord between each group of double rings. Secure the double rings in position with d c, so that they cannot slide out of place, and see that the connecting line of chain is rather shorter than the corresponding cord, so that it makes the cord curve downwards slightly.

2nd Row.—Over each set of double rings, make 2 tr, with 2 ch between, three times over. Then make the same number of ch that is in the line below, catching it with 2 d c in the centre.

3rd Row.—Over the trebles in the row below, make 2 tr with 2 ch between, four times over, and ch 7 between each set.

Now to make the lower edge of the design.

* Into the first opening of the lower part of the rings make 3 tr, 4 ch, 3 tr. Then make 2 tr to grasp the place where the two rings over-wrap, and proceed to make 3 tr, 4 ch, 3 tr in the other side of the second ring. Take 9 ch up to the centre of the curved cross-bar of cord, catching in the centre with 2 d c, 9 ch; this brings you down again to the next set of rings. Repeat from *.

For the next row, into each 4 ch of the previous row, make 2 d c, 4 ch, 2 d c, 4 ch, 2 d c. Then put a d c into each tr in previous row, and again fill the 4 ch of previous row, as just described. Fill the 9 ch of previous row, up and down with d c. Complete row in this way.

For the last row, fill each 4 ch with 7 d c, and carry 7 ch up, and 7 ch down, in the points between the d c rings.

The Ring and Loop Design.

Twist the cord into a ring, taking care to keep it quite a circle when working—a thin part at the bottom, a thick part on each side, and two thin parts crossing at the top. Then make a loop of the cord, and pass it through the ring, as you see it in the illustration, so that it projects below. Secure all firmly together at the thin part, at the top, with d c. Then allowing one section of thick cord for the straight line at the top, proceed to make another ring and loop, securing this firmly; and so on for the length required. You should ch 9, and carry this along the cord between the d c which unite the rings and loops.

Now to make the lower edge.

Make 5 d c into the first open part of the round ring; let the loop of cotton on the hook go round the back of the long loop, then make 5 d c into

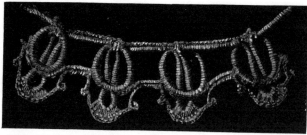

RING AND LOOP DESIGN.

the ring where it crosses the loop;
again catch the thread behind the
long loop, and make another 5 d c in
the next section of the ring. Ch 9,
and start with 5 d c in the next ring,
and in this way complete the row.

For the final row, make * 9 tr into
the bottom of the long loop; ch 8,
catch back into 3rd ch, then make 4
more ch, and catch with a d c into
the 9 ch bar in the previous row. Fill
this bar with 9 d c. Then ch 8, catch
back to 3rd ch, ch 4 and repeat from *.

An Edging for a
Pram Shade.

Use Barbour's F.D.A. Linen Crochet
Thread, No. 18. Start this at the
upper edge. Coil the braid in a
succession of loops ; work from right
to left, make the loops slope to one
side. The braid crosses at the thin
portions. Catch the braid together
in the first place with a sewing needle
and cotton as you go along; these
stitches are afterwards covered with
the crochet.

When a convenient length of these
loops has been made, start at the
lower side of the loops with a d c
over braid where it crosses, making a
d c over each of the two thin parts,
7 ch, a d c into lower point of loop,
7 ch, a d c over the middle of the
thick part of the braid, 7 ch, a d c
over each of the thin parts where the
braid crosses again, 7 ch to point of

next loop. Now make
7 ch, and catch back
from the point of the
one loop into the
middle of thick part
of previous loop, and
return by working
over this connecting
bar of 7 ch, 3 d c, 5 ch,
3 d c, 5 ch, 3 d c. This
brings you back to the point of the loop
again. Continue in this way all
along the length, catching the braid
at the various points indicated with a
d c, and always working 7 ch between,
always remembering the connecting
loop from the point of one loop back
to the middle of the previous loop

Now start a separate piece of work
for the lower portion of the design.
Twist the braid in the pattern seen in
the design having two sets of three
long loops each, one high and the
other lower, alternately. Catch
together firmly at every crossing with
needle and thread and buttonhole-
stitch, Of course, the braid must
always cross at a thin place. Make
the required length of this.

Now starting along the upper side
of this second piece of work, * make
5 d c over the thin part of the braid
on one side where it branches at the
top of the three longest loops, 16 ch to
other side, and another 5 d c in the
thin part. This forms a line across
the top of the V formed by the
braid; then 10 ch along the braid, 2
d c over middle of thick part, 10 ch,
and then put 5 d c altogether over the
part where the three short loops join ;
this will strengthen the parts already
fastened together with sewing cotton.
Proceeding along the upper line of
the work, make 10 ch, catch with 2

d c over centre of thick part of cord, 10 ch, and repeat from *.

The next row unites the narrow strip already made with the lower portion. Into each of the 10 ch in the previous row make 5 d c, 5 ch, 5 d c, the 5 ch forming what looks like little picots. Catch these picots into the similar picots which occur at the lower edge of the narrow strip already made, fill in the 16 ch with 5 d c, 5 ch, 2 d c, 5 ch, 5 d c, catching these picots also to those in the narrow strip.

Now for the bottom of the edging. Start with the longest loops, * into bottom of first loop work 3 d c, 5 ch, 3 d c, ch 9, then into next loop 3 d c, 5 ch, 3 d c, ch 9, and into 3rd loop 3 d c, 5 ch, 3 d c. Now ch 7, and go to the first of the shorter loops; into this make 3 long tr (thread twice over hook), ch 5, 3 long tr into next loop, ch 5, 3 long tr into 3rd short loop. Ch 7, which carries you to next long loop, and repeat from *.

For the next row, into each of the little picot loops made by the 5 ch in the long loops of braid, make 3 loops of 5 ch, then another 5 ch carries you to the connecting bar of 9 ch, fill this with 9 d c. Fill in the ch connecting the shorter braid loops with d c, and also put a d c into the top of each tr in previous row.

In the next row, into each little loop of 5 ch make 3 ordinary trs, with 6 ch between; but make no ch between when you come to the connecting bar of 9 d c; here let the tr go straight on into next loop with no ch between. This is for the bottom of the long braid loops.

At the bottom of the shorter braid loops work 6 ch, 2 d c over the trs, 6 ch, and 2 d c again. Finally fill in each of the little loops of ch with d c, making a little picot-like loop of 5 ch in the centre of each; this applies to the bottom of the long braid loops only. When you reach the shorter braid loops fill in the loops of 6 ch with d c only, omitting the little picot loops made by the 5 ch. The pattern now has a finishing line of ch caught with d c, crocheted along the top, for sewing on.

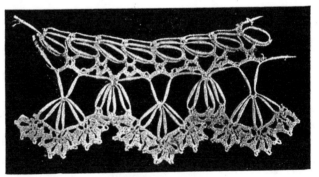

AN EDGING FOR A PRAM SHADE.

A Good Design for Blinds.

This would be very serviceable for toilet-covers, box-covers, valances; or either of the next two designs we give would look well on linen mantel-scarfs. Cream-tinted crochet cotton is necessary to match the tint of the braid.

Begin with the twists of braid running along the top; keep tying the braid into loose cable-like links at the thin part and form in this way a strip; in each case the braid crosses at the thin parts. In the first instance, secure the strands in place with a

With Various Braids.

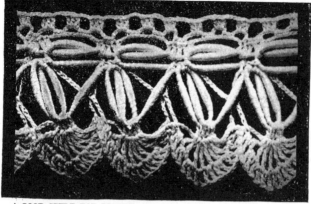

A GOOD STYLE FOR BLINDS
AND FURNISHINGS.

needle and cotton; when a sufficient length of the braid has been twisted, fasten all securely together by making 5 tr over the parts that overlap, catching all the strands together, and then make sufficient chain to reach to the next junction of the braid.

2nd Row.—(At the top of the edging). * Into the three middle tr work 3 d c (one in the top of each tr), then 5 ch, 3 d c (over chain in row below), 5 ch, 3 d c, 5 ch, which brings you to the next set of trs. Repeat from *.

3rd Row.—The sewing-on part is now completed with 3 tr into each of the 5 ch below, and 3 ch between.

The slanting part of the braid-work is now made. Loop the braid much as you did for the top links, but leave a bar in between which slopes to the next link and give a slanting effect to the pattern. Holding the twisted loops in the thumb and fingers, make a d c into each thin part of the braid where it overlaps, and at the same time draw the cotton over the hook and through the thin part in the other edging previously completed (as can be seen by studying the illustration), and in this way unite the two strips of braiding. Ch 16 (which

leave in a loop at the back of the braid) and proceed to fasten the next group together. Complete row in this way.

Now work the scallops at the lower edge of the design.

1st Row.—Into the points of the loops work 4 tr in such a manner as to catch all the strands together, ch 18 and catch together next set of loops.

2nd Row.—* Make a long tr (cotton twice over the hook) into the first of the 4 tr, 3 long tr into the second tr, 3 long tr into the third tr, and one into the last tr, making 2 ch between each tr. After the last tr has been made, ch 2 and catch into the strand of 18 ch. Then ch 5 and catch at the back of the work into the loop of 16 ch previously made, ch 5 and catch once more into the lower strand of 18 ch, then 2 ch and repeat from * all along the row.

3rd Row.—Place into each of the two ch along the previous row, 2 ordinary tr with 1 ch between each, making 1 d c into the centre of the cross strand of 18 ch every time this is reached.

A Small Pincushion Cover with Oval Picot Braid.

Join in a square sixteen ovals of the braid. Four ovals form each side. For the outer border each small scallop is worked separately.

1st Row.—* 1 tr into first loop of scallop, 2 ch, Repeat from * into each loop of scallop; 2 ch, 1 tr over the short bar connecting scallops.

72

2nd Row.—* 4 ch, 2 d c into 2 ch of the previous row. Repeat from * six more times.

3rd Row.—4 ch and 2 tr into 4 ch of 2nd row, * 2 ch, 3 tr into the next 4 ch of 2nd row. Repeat from * five more times.

4th Row.—* 5 ch, 2 d c into 2 ch of 3rd row. Repeat from * six more times.

5th Row.—3 d c into 5 ch of 4th row, place these close together, 4 ch to form a little loop, 3 d c into the same 5 ch of 4th row.

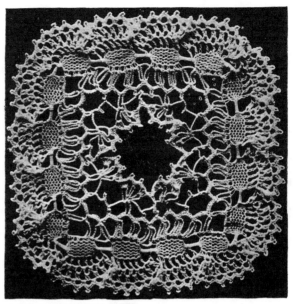

A SMALL PINCUSHION COVER.

The Inner Border of the Square.

1st Row.—1 d c into a loop of the braid about the middle of one side, * 16 ch and 1 d c into the same loop, 1 ch, 1 d c into the next loop. Repeat from * for each scallop, between the scallops a bar of 6 ch to connect them.

When within four loops of the corner, omit the long loop of 16 ch and do * 1 d c into the third loop of scallop, 1 ch. Repeat from * to the end of the side.

Commence the next side by * 1 d c into 1st loop, 1 ch. Repeat from * for 4 loops, then * 1 d c into 5th loop, 16 ch, 1 d c into 5th loop, 1 ch. * Repeat from * with a bar of 6 ch between the scallops.

2nd Row.—1 d c into 2nd long loop of the 2nd scallop of the 1st row, 1 d c into 3rd loop of the same scallop, 6 ch, 1 d c into 4th loop, 1 d c into 5th loop, 6 ch, 1 d c into 6th loop, 1 d c into 1st loop of next scallop. Continue along the four sides of the square; when the corner is reached do 1 d c into the last loop of that side, 1 d c into the 1st loop of the next side.

3rd Row.—Commence at a corner 6 d c over 1st ch 6 of the 2nd row, * 3 d c over 2nd 6 ch of 2nd row, 5 ch to form a small loop, 3 d c over the same 6 ch, 3 d c over 3rd 6 ch of previous line, 12 ch to form a long loop, 3 d c into same 6 ch, 3 d c over next 6 ch, 5 ch, 3 d c, 3 d c over next 6 ch, 5 ch, 3 d c, 3 d c over next 6 ch, 12 ch, 3 d c, 3 d c over next 6 ch, 5 ch, 3 d c, 6 d c over last 6 ch of previous bar. Repeat along each of the three remaining sides.

4th Row.—1 d c into 1st long loop of 3rd row, 12 ch, 1 d c, 12 ch, 1 d c, 12 ch, 1 d c, making three long loops, 6 ch, 1 d c into 1st short loop, 14 ch, 1 d c into 5 ch of this 14 to form a picot, 4 ch, 1 d c into 2nd short loop. Connect the short and long loops in this way until the 4th row is completed.

5th Row.—4 tr into 1st long loop of 4th row, * 5 ch, 1 d c into 2nd loop, 5 ch, 3 tr into 3rd loop, 5 ch, 1 d c into picot loop of 4th row, 5 ch, 4 tr into next long loop. Repeat from *.

6th Row.—Commence at a corner 5 d c, * 5 ch to form a loop, 5 d c, 5 ch, 12 d c, 5 ch to form a loop, 5 d c, 5 ch to form a loop, 12 d c. Repeat from *.

A Useful Pattern
for Hard Wear.

For this use Barbour's No. 30 F.D.A. Linen Crochet Thread.

1st Row.—Connect the little loops of the first oval of the braid by 1 d c into the first loop, * 2 ch, 1 d c into the next loop. Repeat from * 5 more times. The 6 ch into the 1st loop of the next oval, 1 tr, * 2 ch, 1 tr. Repeat 5 more times from *.

2nd Row.—1st Oval. 1 d c over each 2 ch of 1st row, 2 ch between 6 d c

over bar of 6 ch of previous row, 4 ch, 2 d c into each 2 ch of 2nd oval, 2 ch between.

3rd Row.—1st Oval. 1 d c over each 2 ch of previous line, 2 ch between ; this will be done 6 times altogether. 6 ch, 2 tr into 1st 4 ch of 2nd oval. * 2 ch, 2 tr into next 4 ch. Repeat from * 4 more times.

4th Row.—1st Oval. 1 d c over 2 ch of 3rd row, 2 ch, 1 d c over next 2 ch. 5 times altogether. 6 d c over previous bar of 6 ch, * 4 ch, then 2 d c into 2 ch of 2nd oval of previous row, 4 ch, 2 d c. Repeat 4 more times.

5th Row.—1st Oval. 1 d c over 2 ch of previous row, 2 ch, 1 d c over the next 2 ch. 5 times altogether. 7 ch, 3 tr into 4 ch of 2nd oval of previous row, * 2 ch, 3 tr. Repeat from * 4 more times.

6th Row.—1st Oval. 1 d c into the 1st 2 ch of 5th row, 2 ch, 1 d c into next 2 ch. 4 times altogether. 7 d c over the bar of 7 ch, 5 ch, * 2 d c into 2 ch of previous line, 5 ch. Repeat from * 4 more times.

7th Row.—1st Oval. 1 d c into the 1st 2 ch of 6th row, 2 ch, 1 d c into the next 2 ch, 2 ch, 1 d c into the next 2 ch of 6th row, 7 ch, * 4 tr into 5 ch of 2nd oval of 5th row, 2 ch. Repeat from * 5 times.

8th Row.—1 d c into 2 ch of 1st oval, 2 ch, 1 d c, 7 d c over

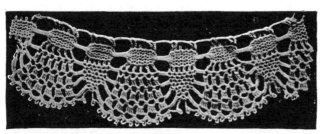

A USEFUL PATTERN FOR HARD WEAR.

SHOWING THE PATTERN BOTH SIDES OF THE BRAID.

bar of **7** ch of 7th row, * **7** ch, **2** d c into **2** ch of 2nd oval of 7th row. Repeat from * **5** times.

9th Row.—Into each **7** ch of 8th row **2** d c, then * **6** ch, **3** d c, **6** ch, **2** d c (each **6** ch forms a little ring). When each group of **7** ch is finished, do **10** ch, catch back into 5th to form a loop. **5** ch, **1** d c into the **2** ch of 1st oval of 8th line, **10** ch; catch back into 5th, **5** ch, **2** d c into next **7** ch of previous line. Repeat from *.

Below this is shown a similar pattern worked both sides of the braid. This makes a handsome insertion.

A Fine Edging in Picot Braid.

For this lace select lace braid having **6** picots at each side of the oval. Form the braid into downward loops of **4** ovals each by crossing the braid at the bars, where they are secured with a few tight stitches, leaving **2** ovals at the top between the loops.

Use Barbour's No. **70** Linen Lace Thread.

1st Row.—At the top, into the 1st picot on the 1st of the two bars between the loops **1** long tr, * **3** ch, **2** tr into each of the 3rd and 4th picots, **3** ch, **2** tr into the 6th picot, **5** ch, **2** tr into 1st picot on next oval, **3** ch, **2** tr into each of 3rd and 4th picots, **3** ch,

1 long tr into 6th picot, **1** long tr into 1st picot on next oval, then repeat from *.

2nd Row.—* **2** tr between the tr on centre of oval, **3** ch, **2** tr into next **2** tr, **5** ch, **2** tr into next **2** tr, **5** ch, **2** tr into centre of tr on oval, **5** ch, **1** long tr between next long tr, **5** ch and repeat from *.

At the lower edge commence on the 1st of the 4 ovals that form the loop.

1st Row.—**2** tr into each of the last **3** picots on 1st oval, * **7** ch, **2** d c over the bar, **7** ch, **2** tr into each of next **6** picots and repeat from * twice, as far as the **2** tr into the 3rd picot on the 4th loop, cross over to the last 3 picots on next oval and put **2** tr into each, **2** tr into each of first 3 picots on next oval, then repeat from the beginning.

2nd Row.—**2** tr into sp between tr into 1st oval in 5th and 6th picots, * **7** tr over next ch, **3** ch, **7** tr over next ch, **2** ch, **2** tr into sp between 1st and 2nd picots on next oval, **5** ch, **1** d c into sp between the 3rd and 4th picots, **5** ch, **2** tr between 5th and 6th picots, **2** ch, repeat from * twice, omitting the last **2** ch, cross over to next loop and repeat from the beginning.

3rd Row.—**7** tr into the sp between the **7** tr in last row, **7** ch, picot 5 of them, **2** ch, **2** d c over next **2** ch, **3** d c, **5** ch, **3** d c into each of next **2** sp, **2** d c over next **2** ch, **7** ch, picot 5 of them, **2** ch, and repeat from the beginning once, **7** tr over ch between next **7** tr, cross over to the opposite side with **7** tr into the corresponding sp and repeat from the beginning.

With Various Braids.

Picot Braid with Coarse Cotton.

Coarse picot braid with Ardern's No. 24 crochet cotton.

Form downward loops of 4 ovals each by crossing the braid at the bars and secure with a few neat stitches on the back, leave 2 ovals between the loops.

PICOT BRAID WITH COARSE COTTON.

1st Row.—Into each of last 3 picots on 1st oval put 1 d c, 2 ch between, over next bar, * 2 d c, 7 ch, 1 d c, 12 ch, 1 d c, 7 ch, 2 d c, 1 d c into next picot, 3 ch, 3 tr into each of next 4, 3 ch, 1 d c into next, repeat from * into the bar, next oval and following bar, 1 d c into each of next 3 picots with 2 ch between, repeat into last 3 picots on next oval, 6 ch, 1 d c over next bar, 6 ch, 1 d c into each of next 3 picots with 2 ch between, and repeat.

2nd Row.—* 5 d c into the top of each loop of ch, into the sp between the tr into 2nd and 3rd picots on next oval 4 long tr, 5 ch, 2 long tr, 5 ch, 2 long tr, 5 ch, 4 long tr, into each of next 3 loops 4 long tr with 5 ch between, turn back after the last tr, 5 ch, 3 d c, 5 ch, 3 d c into space between tr, 5 ch, 3 d c, 5 ch, 3 d c into next space, 5 ch, 1 d c, before 1st long tr of next 4, turn, and repeat the groups of long tr into the 3 top spaces, catching up the 5 ch picot between each set, then into the sp over the next oval, 5 d c into each ch loop, cross over to opposite loop and repeat from * catching in the d c at the opposite side in the centre.

For the heading, * 2 tr into each of 1st 2 picots, 3 ch, 2 tr into 4th picot, 3 ch, 2 tr into 6th picot (use long tr for these and following 2) 4 ch over the crossing bars, 2 long tr into next picot, 3 ch, 2 tr into 3rd picot, 3 ch, 2 tr into each of 5th and 6th picots, 4 ch and repeat from *.

A Butterfly D'oiley Design.

Use Barbour's No. 36 F.D.A. Linen Crochet Thread. Cross the braid and tack in place. Fill in middles with loops of ch worked from a centre ring of 4 ch. The longer loops have 9 ch, the shorter 6 ch.

Round the outside edge work loops of 4 ch with 1 d c between, doing 4 rows.

A BUTTERFLY D'OILEY DESIGN.

At every point in 1st row do 4 long tr with 4 ch between, into thick part of braid, the first and last cotton twice round hook, the 2 centre ones cotton 3 times round hook. For picot edge do 1 d c in loop, 7 ch, catch back to 2nd ch for picot, 2 ch, 1 d c in next loop and repeat.

To straighten inner edge do 3 loops of 4 ch across thick part of braid, 12 ch, catch to 8th to form ring, 6 ch, 1 d c into 2 centre loops of braid, 6 ch back to ring, 9 ch, 1 d c into 2 bottom loops of braid, 9 ch back to ring, 6 ch, 1 d c into 2 centre loops of braid, 6 ch back to ring, 7 ch, 1 d c in top loop of braid, and continue all round. Do 4 or 5 rows of loops of 4 ch, skipping a loop in 3rd round in every pattern to shape it. Then 3 ch and 1 tr in every loop to finish d'oiley.

Irish Shamrocks with a Fancy Braid.

This design is suitable for ornamenting household napery of all kinds.

Use Barbour's No. 45 F.D.A. Linen Crochet Thread.

Take a yard length of the cotton, fold it in two, and fasten the crochet thread to the folded end with a d c, twist the folded thread round to form a ring and work 24 d c into it. 1 d c into the 1st on ring, 5 ch, 1 d c into each of the next 5 d c on ring, * 7 ch to turn, 1 d c into 1st loop, 5 ch, 1 d c into each loop of last row *, repeat 3 times, work 2 more rows of loops but decrease 1 at each side, then put a loop into each down the side to the centre, 8 d c into next 8 on ring, turn, 2 d c into last d c, 1 d c into each of next 4, 2 d c into next, turn and repeat this row, putting 2 d c into the first and last of each row, until 10 rows are formed, then decrease at the beginning and end of next 3 rows, slipstitch to the ring, 4 d c into next 4 on ring, 5 ch, 1 d c into each of next 6 d c on ring, turn and repeat 1st leaflet. Take up the padding thread and lay it along the edge of the 1st leaflet and work d s closely over it into each sp all round, then round the centre leaflet and last. Continue working d c over the padding alone for 30 stitches, turn, miss 2 and work a 2nd row into the 1st. Fasten the padding securely on the back. Make a ring of the padding thread and work d c over it, sew this ring over the centre, neatly and securely. The stem is connected with the leaflet by a single row of picot loops, and the shamrocks are then sewn to each other and to the braid in the order illustrated. Finish with a row of trs into every 2nd picot on the braid, alternating with 2 ch. Over the ch stitches work 4 d c into each sp.

An Edge with Fine Braid.
Lower Edge.

1st Row.—2 tr into 1st loop of the braid, * 2 ch, 2 tr into next loop.

IRISH SHAMROCKS WITH FANCY BRAID.

77

With Various Braids.

Repeat from * 7 times, miss 12 loops, 2 tr into 22nd loop, * 2 ch, 2 tr into next loop. Repeat from *, miss 12 loops, 2 tr into the next loop, * 2 ch, 2 tr into next loop. Repeat from * 7 times, miss 12 loops, 2 tr into the next loop, 3 ch, miss one loop, 2 tr into the next. Repeat 6 times, miss 12 loops and repeat from the beginning of the directions.

2nd Row.—1 d c into 1st tr of 1st row, 9 ch, 1 d c between 2nd and 3rd tr of 1st row, * 9 ch, 1 d c between 4th and 5th tr, 7 ch, 1 d c between the 5th and 6th tr, 9 ch, 1 d c between the 7th, 8 tr, 5 ch, 1 d c between the 2nd and 3rd tr of the next point of scallop. Repeat from * twice

AN EDGE WITH FINE BRAID.

5 ch, 1 d c between the 2nd and 3rd tr of straight part, 9 ch, 1 d c between 4th and 5th tr, 9 ch, 1 d c between 6th and 7th tr, 5 ch, 1 d c between 2nd and 3rd tr of the next scallop.

3rd Row.—Make an edge of small loops of 9 ch, then 1 d c. Over the 5 ch of 2nd row that connects the points of the scallops 6 d c.

Upper Edge.

1st Row.—Along the straight parts of the braid 2 tr into the first loop, * 2 ch, miss 1 loop, 2 tr into the next loop. Repeat from * 9 times, 5 ch, miss 1 loop, 1 d c, 1 ch into the next loop, * 1 ch, 1 d c into the next loop.

Repeat from * 4 times, miss 12 loops, * 1 d c, 1 ch. Repeat from * 5 times.

Miss about 16 loops, and at the top of the next point * 1 d c, 1 ch. Repeat from * 5 times. Miss about 10 loops, * 1 d c, 1 ch. Repeat from * 5 times, 5 ch, miss 1 loop, 2 tr into next loop. Repeat from the beginning of the 1st row.

2nd Row.—Above the line of 2 tr, 2 ch of previous row, 2 tr into each 2 ch and 2 ch between. After the 10th 2 tr, 7 ch, 6 d c over the 5th ch of 1st row, 5 ch. Miss the 1st line of 1 d c, 1 ch, and between the 3rd and 4th d c of the 2nd row of 1 d c, 1 ch, 2 long tr, 1 ch, 2 long tr between the 4th and 5th d c, 1 ch, 2 long trs between the 3rd and 4th d c of 3rd row of 1 d c, 1 ch; then make 1 ch, 2 long tr between the 4th and 5th dc. Miss the next row of 1 d c, 1 ch, 5 ch, 6 d c over 5 ch, of previous line, 5 ch. Continue from the beginning of the 2nd row.

3rd Row.—Above the straight row of tr and ch do 4 tr into the 1st bar of ch, 5 ch, 4 tr into the next bar, * 5 ch, miss 1 bar, 4 tr into the next. Repeat from * 3 times, 5 ch, 4 tr into next bar of ch. 5 ch, 1 long tr before long tr of 2nd row, 1 long tr between 2nd and 3rd, 1 long tr between 4th and 5th, 1 long tr between 6th and 7th, 1 long tr after the 8th long tr of the 2nd row, 5 ch. Continue from the beginning of the 3rd row.

4th Row.—Above each group of 4 tr do 2 tr with 7 ch between, above the group of 5 long tr do 2 long tr.

A LIGHT TRIMMING AND LOOP EDGING
SHOWING THE BRAIDS USED.

A Light Trimming
with Mignardise Braid.

For this pretty trimming use fine fancy Mignardise braid, as illustrated, with No. 60 crochet cotton.

For the Heading.

Into first picot 2 tr, 2 ch, * 2 tr into next picot, 3 ch, 1 tr into each of next two picots, 3 ch, 2 tr into next picot, 2 ch, * repeat to the end.

1st Row of Edging.—2 tr into first picot, 2 ch, 2 tr into second picot, 2 ch, 2 tr into third picot, * miss next picot, 8 ch, 2 tr into next picot, 2 ch, 2 tr into next, 2 ch, 2 tr into next, * repeat to the end.

2nd Row.—* 3 d c into the 2 ch space, 2 ch, 3 d c into next space, 7 ch, 4 tr over the 8 ch, 7 ch, * repeat to the end.

3rd Row.—* 3 d c into the 2 ch space, 9 ch, 3 tr before next 4 tr of last row, 3 ch, 3 tr after the 4 tr, 9 ch, * repeat.

4th Row.—* 2 d c over the 9 ch, 5 ch, 6 long tr (thread 3 times over), with 2 ch between into the space between the trs, 5 ch, 2 d c over next 9 ch, 5 ch, * repeat.

5th Row.—* 2 d c into the space before the long trs, 4 ch, 2 d c into each space between the trs, 4 ch, 2 d c after the trs, 4 ch, 5 d c over next 5 ch, 4 ch, * repeat.

Loop Edging in
Braid and Crochet.

A plain and a fancy Mignardise braid are used for this lace, with No. 60 crochet cotton.

Commence by preparing the upper row of fancy braid for the heading by putting 1 tr, 3 ch into every picot.

With the plain Mignardise form downward loops, one large, one small alternating ; in the small loop enclose 23 picots and in the large 35, cross the braid and secure in place on the back with a few neat stitches, in such a way as to leave 8 picots on the upper side entirely free. Into the third picot on the right of the first loop fasten the thread with a d c, 2 ch, 1 d c into each of next 5 picots, 5 tr into next picot, 5 ch, 1 d c into second next picot, 5 ch, 5 tr into second next picot, 1 d c into next, 2 ch, 1 d c into each of next 5, 4 tr into the four centre picots of the braid between the loops, cross over to the third picot on the large loop with a d c, 2 ch, 1 d c into each of next 9 picots, catching in the opposite side in the fourth 2 ch, 5 tr into next, 5 ch, 1 d c into second next picot, 5 ch, 5 tr into second next picot, 5 ch, 1 d c into second next picot,

With Various Braids.

5 ch, 5 tr into second next picot, 1 d c into next, 2 ch, 1 d c into each of next 9 picots, 4 tr into 4 centre picots on the braid, then repeat from the beginning, catching in the sides in the fourth 2 ch.

For the top portion of the loops, * 1 d c into the two picots over the crossing of the braid in the loop, 3 ch, 2 tr into the second of the 8 picots on the braid, 3 ch, 2 tr into fourth picot, 5 ch, 2 tr into fifth picot, 3 ch, 2 tr into seventh picot, 3 ch, 1 d c into the two picots over next crossing, repeating from *.

2nd Row.—* 3 d c over the 3 ch, 5 tr into next space, 1 d c over the 5 ch, catch in a picot on the heading, 2 d c into same space, and catch in next picot on heading, 1 d c into same space, 5 tr into next space, 3 d c into next, repeat from *, catching in the heading in the next third and fourth picots.

tr on the needle until finishing the 3rd, then work off all together, 4 ch, 3 tr into each 3rd picot until 12 groups are formed, * 4 ch, 1 d c into next 3rd picot, draw the thread through next 3rd picot and make a ch stitch, repeat through every 3rd picot until there are 12 ch on the needle, make a d c through all, drawing it up tight, then cross the braid on the back and secure with a d c, 4 ch, 3 tr into every 2nd picot until 12 groups are formed, 4 ch, 1 d c into 2nd next picot, 4 ch, 3 tr into each of next four 2nd picots, 4 ch, 1 d c into 2nd next picot, 4 ch, 3 tr into each of next two 2nd picots, 1 ch, 3 tr into the centre of the 4 groups between the d c, 1 ch, 1 d c into the loop after the 10th group of tr, 2 ch, 3 tr into 2nd next picot.

Continue forming the groups of tr down this side, joining to the opposite side in the centre of the loop until

A Handsome Circular Crochet Lace.

This would be used for d'oileys, and lamp or candle-shades.

Fine narrow picot braid is required, with Man-love's No. 50 Crochet Cotton and a No. 7 hook.

Note.—The trs throughout this design are to be "long trebles."

1 d c into 1st picot, 4 ch, 3 tr into 3rd picot, retain the last loop in each

A HANDSOME CIRCULAR CROCHET LACE.

six joinings are made; continue the group of tr with 4 ch between until 5 more are formed, that is 12 in all from the d c at the top.

Repeat from * connecting the top corners at the 1st d c through the picot opposite the d c at the corresponding side of last corner.

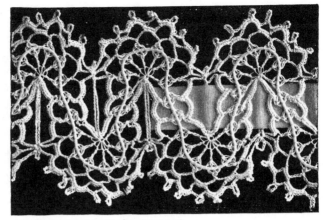

A FINE CROCHET LACE FOR LINGERIE.

To fill in the centre, ch 6, form into a ring into which put 12 d c, 1 single through the first d c, * 6 ch, fasten with a d c to the centre picot in the oval, 6 ch 1 d c into next on ring, 6 ch 1 d c into next 4th picot, 6 ch, 1 d c into next on ring, 9 ch 1 d c into next 4th picot, 9 ch 1 d c into next on ring, 9 ch 1 d c into the corresponding picot at opposite side, 9 ch 1 d c into next on ring, 6 ch 1 d c into next 4th picot, 6 ch 1 d c into next on ring, 6 ch 1 d c into next 4th picot, 6 ch, 1 d c into next on ring, then repeat from *.

For the edging put 2 d c, 5 ch, 2 d c into each 4 ch sp. 1 d c into 2nd picot on the circle, 7 ch, picot 5 of them, 2 ch, 1 d c into every 2nd picot on circle to the second last, then cross over to the next 4 ch between the groups of tr and repeat, putting a 5 ch picot over the last joining between the motifs, and 2 d c on each half bar.

A Fine Crochet Lace for Lingerie.

Use fine picot braid with No. 50 Ardern's crochet cotton.

Commence with * 8 ch, take up next 3 picots on the hook and make a d c through them, repeat from * 9 times more. 8 ch, 1 long tr into next 3 together, retain the last loop on the needle in this and following trs, repeat the tr 6 times more into next picots, taking up 3 with each, then thread through all the loops on needle, drawing them up closely with a d c. Repeat from the 1st 8 ch until a sufficient length is made.

2nd Row.—8 d c over the 1st, 2nd and 3rd 8 ch, 8 ch, 5 d c into next 5 loops, 8 ch, 8 d c into each of next 3 loops, 1 d c into the centre of the circle, 16 ch, fasten to the centre of last 8 ch loop with a d c, 16 ch, 1 d c into circle, 8 d c into each of next loops, 4 ch, 1 d c into the d c fastening the 16 ch to loop at opposite side, 4 ch, 5 d c into next loop, then repeat from *.

3rd Row.—Fasten the thread to the 1st 8 ch loop, * 6 ch picot into top of loop, 4 ch, 4 d c, 6 ch picot, 4 d c into each of next 4 loops, with 8 ch picot 6 of them, 2 ch, between the loops over the 5 d c, 4 ch, 1 d c into the joining where a picot is made as at first, then repeat from *.

The other side is worked in the same way, reversing the loops and circles, taking care to have the trs in

With Various Braids.

TABLE CENTRE WITH EFFECTIVE
BRAID AND CROCHET WHEELS.

the circle exactly in the centre of the 11 open loops on the other side. The 16 ch bars support the lingerie ribbon run through the centre.

Table Centre with Braid and Crochet Wheels.

Use fine picot braid and Ardern's No. 50 crochet cotton.

Fasten the thread with a d c to a picot at the end of the braid, make a ch stitch through every 2nd picot for 5 stitches, which you retain on the hook, * thread over needle and through all on needle, draw the stitch up tight to form a semicircle of the braid, 2 ch, cross over behind the braid to next picot at opposite side, into which put 1 d c, 7 ch, miss next 5 picots, and put a triple tr into every 2nd picot for 12 tr, retaining the last loop in each on the needle, draw the thread through all the loops on the needle and close up tight, 7 ch, miss next 5 picots and put the needle through the 6th and the picot at the beginning of the 1st 7 ch, make a single, 2 ch, cross behind the braid to next picot at opposite side, into which make 1 ch and 1 ch into each of next 5 2nd picots, then repeat from *.

Form 8 of the large loops, then join the ends of the braid neatly after closing the motif, ch 8 and form into a ring, into which put 16 d c, 1 single through the 1st d c, * 3 ch fasten with a d c to the centre picot on the inner semicircle, 3 ch 1 d c into next on ring, then repeat from * into next semicircle and all round.

Eight of these motifs are required, and when all are worked place them on a linen centre-piece after the manner illustrated, and mark the linen for the inner edge, taking care to have the curves equal. Work a row of buttonhole-stitch around the centre.

Fasten the thread to the outer edge of one of the motifs * at the picot opposite the 2nd triple tr, 3 ch 1 d c into every 2nd picot to 2nd last tr, cross over to next mitre and repeat from * over next 7 mitres, cross over to 1st mitre and work 4 d c into each of the spaces on 4 mitres, into each of last 4 put * 4 d c into 1st 2 spaces, 2 d c into next, 4 ch, turn these back and fasten to last 5th d c, turn, 2 d c, 5 ch, 2 d c, 5 ch, 2 d c into the loop, repeat from * over the mitre, and into next 3.

Two of the mitres with a half-mitre at each side should fit into the edge of the linen to which the lace is neatly top-sewn, and the remaining halves of the mitres at each side are joined together where they meet only.

Braid and Crochet D'oiley.

Use fine picot braid and Manlove's No. 42 Irish Lace Thread.

Commence with 3 long tr into one

BRAID AND CROCHET D'OILEY.

of the picots, retaining the last loop of each on the needle until all are worked, then thread through all together, * 6 ch, 3 long tr into 2nd next picot * until 10 groups are formed, 1 long tr into 2nd next picot (retaining the last loop) twice, work off 2 loops together, repeat six times more, join first and last of these 7 groups of 2 tr with a d c, then repeat from * at the beginning, connecting the sides at the centre of the 2nd ch space.

2nd Row, lower edge.—Over the 3rd space make 3 long tr as before, * 2 ch, 3 long tr, 6 ch, 3 long tr into next space, * repeat into next 2 spaces, 2 ch, 3 long tr into next space, then repeat from the beginning.

3rd Row.—1 d c over each 2 ch and 10 tr over each 6 ch.

For the 1st inner row, commence at the first picot after the first 3 tr at opposite side with * a tr, 1 tr into every 2nd picot 8 times more, join first and last with a single, 7 ch, 1 d c into next 7th picot, 3 ch, 1 tr into every 2nd picot 8 times, 3 ch, 1 d c into 2nd next picot, 7 ch, miss 6 picots, and repeat from * into next, join the end of next 7 ch to the beginning of the last with 1 d c.

4th Row.—* 1 d c into top centre space, 5 ch, 1 long tr into next space but one, 1 long tr into corresponding space on next mitre, 5 ch, repeat from *

Join the ends neatly, and top-sew to the linen centre, which has been cut to the required size, neatly hemmed, and a row of feather-stitch worked over the edge of the hem.

DESIGNS FOR MATS AND PINCUSHION TOPS.

A LOVELY MAT OR D'OILEY

A Lovely Mat or D'oiley.

Ardern's No. 40 crochet cotton is required for this design. Commence with 120 ch formed into a ring, into every fifth ch put a loop composed of 10 ch, picot 5 of them, 5 ch, fasten with a d c, 24 loops in all, 5 d c into each ch space on the inside. Into each picot put 3 loops of 18 ch each with 16 ch between the picots.

In the next row, * 1 d c into the top of each loop on the first 4 picots, and 1 d c in the centre of the ch between, 10 ch, picot 5 of them, 5 ch 1 d c into next loop, 10 ch, picot 5 of them, 5 ch 1 d c into top of next 3 loops, 10 ch, picot 5 of them, 5 ch 1 d c into next loop, 10 ch, picot 5 of them, 5 ch 1 d c into each of next 3 loops, 10 ch, picot 5 of them, 5 ch 1 d c into next loop, 10 ch, picot 5 of them, 5 ch and repeat from *, thus forming a square.

Motif Insertion.

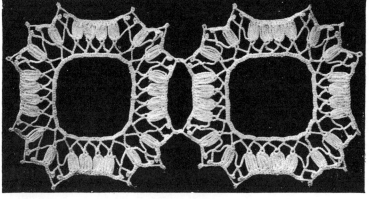

THIS INSERTION IS FORMED BY JOINING SEVERAL OF THE SQUARES SHOWN IN THE CENTRE OF THE PREVIOUS DESIGN.

Around the square, 1 d c into each of first consecutive d c, 4 d c into next sp, 10 ch, picot 5 of them, 5 ch, 4 d c into next loop after the picot, 1 d c into each of next d c, 4 d c over next loop, 10 ch, picot 5 of them, 5 ch, 4 d c into next loop after the picot, 1 d c into each of next d c, 4 d c into next loop, 10 ch, picot 5 of them, 5 ch, 4 d c over next loop after the picot. Repeat from * three times more.

Into each picot all round a figure is formed of 9 loops of 18 ch each fastened with a d c, 9 ch, turn, 5 ch 1 d c into each loop, * turn, 2 ch 1 d c into first loop, 5 ch 1 d c into each loop, repeat from * until only one loop remains, slip stitch down to the first long loop and turning, put 3 d c 4 ch 3 d c into every second loop up the side and into the point with 3 d c into the intervening loops.

Connect the figures in the last picot at each side, all round, and in the second picots also in the two figures at each side of the square. For the outer edging fasten the thread to the second picot, on the corner figure, 16 ch, 1 d c into next picot, 18 ch 1 d c into same picot three times, repeat from the beginning into each of next 4 picots, 16 ch 1 d c into next picot,

cross over with 3 ch to next picot and repeat around the figure, omitting the last three loops and putting 1 d c into the picot instead. 5 ch 1 d c into next picot, 5 ch 1 d c into the picots at the connection, 5 ch 1 d c into next picot on next figure, 1 d c through the picot opposite, 5 ch 1 d c into next picot, 16 ch 1 d c into next picot where the three loops are repeated and into the following three picots, 16 ch, 1 d c into next picot, cross over to next picot with 3 ch and repeat from the first.

Last Row.—8 d c over first chs, * 8 ch 1 d c into each on loops, 8 ch 1 d c into each loop between, * repeat, ending with 8 d c over last chs, 3 d c over the 3 ch, then repeat from the beginning. Finish with 8 d c over each 8 ch with no ch between, 4 d c at each side of a group of loops and a picot loop between the groups, each loop composed as before of 10 ch, picot 5 of them, 5 ch.

The squares shown above are worked exactly like the centre of the larger one.

Guelder Rose Design for a Pin-cushion Top.

Use Barbour's No. 40 Linen Lace Thread, and make 10 ch into a ring, into the ring put 10 tr, 5 ch, 10 tr.

2nd Row.—3 ch, 1 tr into each tr, 5 ch, 1 d c into the 5 ch sp, 5 ch, 1 tr into each tr.

85

For Mats and Pincushion Tops.

3rd and 4th Rows.—Same as 2nd.

5th Row.—5 tr into first 5 tr, 5 ch, 5 tr into next 5 tr, 5 ch, 1 d c into each 5 ch loop, 5 ch, 5 tr into next 5 tr, 5 ch, 5 tr into next 5 tr.

Repeat the 5th row four times more, the number of 5 ch loops between the trs increases by one in each row. In the last row put 10 ch in the centre loop, that is, the loop immediately over the 10 ch ring in the beginning.

Connect 8 of these motifs in the 2nd, 3rd, 4th and 5th loops at the side, while making the 2nd and succeeding motifs.

Every 2nd motif only requires the 10 ch in the centre loop.

Into this loop is worked a similar motif, that is, four in the inner row; they are joined in the last row to each other as in the first row, and to that row in the first and last trs to the 3rd loop from each side of the centre loops.

GUELDER ROSE DESIGN.

SQUARE PIN-CUSHION TOP.

Square Pin-cushion Top.

Use Manlove's No. 42 thread for
this square, which is composed of four
strips of insertion and four corner
motifs.

For the insertion commence with
26 ch, turn.

1st Row.—1 tr into the 18th ch, 2 ch,
1 tr into every 3rd ch to the end.

2nd Row.—Turn, with 5 ch at the
beginning of every row, 1 tr into 2nd
tr of first row and into each of the
following 15 stitches, 2 ch, 1 tr into
the 3rd next ch, turn.

3rd Row.—* 4 tr into next 4 consecutive trs, 3 spaces (a space consists
of 2 ch followed by a tr into the next
3rd stitch), 3 tr into next 3, 2 ch, 1 tr
into next 3rd ch.

4th Row.—10 tr into next 10 stitches
1 sp, 4 tr into next 4, 2 ch, 1 tr into
next 3rd ch.

5th Row.—4 tr into next 4, 3 sp, 4 tr
into last 4, 2 ch, 1 tr into next 3rd ch.

6th Row.—4 tr into next 4, 1 sp, 10
tr into next 10 stitches, 2 ch, 1 tr into
next 3rd ch, * repeat until there are
29 rows from the beginning; in the
next row put 1 sp, 16 tr, 1 sp, and in
the last row make 7 sp as at the
beginning. Make four of these strips.

The Corner Motif.

38 ch, turn.

1st Row.—1 tr into the 30th ch, 2 ch,
1 tr into every 3rd ch, turn with 5 ch
at each end.

2nd Row.—3 sp, 7 tr, 6 sp.

For Mats and Pincushion Tops.

3rd Row.— 2 sp, 4 tr, 2 sp, 4 tr, 2 sp, 4 tr, 2 sp.

4th Row.—3 sp, 4 tr, 1 sp, 4 tr, 1 sp, 4 tr, 1 sp, 4 tr, 1 sp.

5th Row.—1 sp, 4 tr, 3 sp, 4 tr, 5 sp.

6th Row.—2 sp, 10 tr, 1 sp, 10 tr, 2 sp.

7th Row.—5 sp, 4 tr, 3 sp, 4 tr, 1 sp.

8th Row.—1 sp, 4 tr, 1 sp, 4 tr, 1 sp, 4 tr, 1 sp, 4 tr, 3 sp.

9th Row.—2 sp, 4 tr, 2 sp, 4 tr, 2 sp, 4 tr, 2 sp.

10th Row.—6 sp, 7 tr, 3 sp.

11th Row.—11 sp.

Make four of these motifs. Take one of the strips and work a row of 3 d c into each sp at one side, take a motif and connect with the strip by working a row of d c over the edges of the 7 sp in both together, then join the other sides in the same way. On the outside of the square work a row of sp all round, putting the trs into the d c over the trs in the sp below.

The Edging.

3 d c into each of first 3 sp on a strip, * 3 tr into next sp, 3 long tr into next ; into next sp 3 triple tr, 5 ch, 3 triple tr, 3 long tr into next sp, 3 tr into next, 3 d c into next, * repeat to the end, work d c into the spaces to the corner of the motif and into next 3 spaces on the end, then repeat the trs, work down the other side to correspond, then repeat from the beginning.

2nd Row.—Fasten the thread to the d c over the second last tr on the motif where it joins the strip, 7 ch, 1 d c into next tr and following 5 tr, * 7 ch, 5 long tr into next space, 7 ch, 1 d c, 7 ch, 5 long tr all into the same space as last, 7 ch, 1 d c into each of the next 4th, 5th and 6th tr, 3 ch, cross over to opposite tr and form a d c, 1 d c into each of next 2 tr, then repeat from *, finishing the strip to correspond with the beginning.

7 ch, 1 d c into the corner d c, 7 ch, 1 d c over second next tr, 7 ch, 1 d c into next 4th, 5th and 6th tr, 7 ch, into next space put 5 long trs, 7 ch, 5 long trs, then work down the side to correspond with the first and repeat all round.

3rd Row.—4 d c over the 7 ch, 7 ch, 3 long tr over same ch, * 4 d c over end of next ch, 1 d c into each tr, 3 d c over next ch, 8 ch, picot 4 of them, 4 ch, 3 d c over ch and 1 d c into each tr, 4 d c over next ch, 3 long tr over the 4 ch and repeat from *, finishing the corner as at the beginning. 5 d c, 5 ch, 5 d c over each of next two 7 ch, then repeat as over preceding trs, and work each corner of the motifs in the same way.

For the Inner Side of the Square.

1st Row.—3 d c into each of first 4 sp, 2 d c, 7 ch, 2 d c into next sp, 3 d c into next, 2 d c, 7 ch, 2 d c into next, 3 d c into each of next 3, 2 d c, 7 ch, 2 d c into next, 3 d c into next, 2 d c, 7 ch, 2 d c into next, 3 d c into each of next 5 sp, then finish the last half to correspond with the first and work the other three sides in the same way.

2nd Row.—3 d c into the 3 d c over the 3rd sp. * 7 ch, 3 long tr into next picot, 2 ch, 3 long tr into next picot, 7 ch, 3 d c into the d c over next 3rd sp, * repeat, and cross over the corner with 5 ch to next 3rd sp.

3rd Row.—Work d c closely over the ch and put a 5 ch picot at the beginning of the 3 tr, over the ch between, and after each of last 3.

Section VII.

FILET MESH CROCHET.

Filet Mesh Crochet.

Workers vary slightly in their methods of Filet Crochet, but the result sought for is the same in all cases, square meshes of solid and of open work.

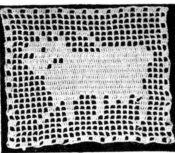

THE COW.

According to the general plan of Filet Crochet Work, 3 ch should be made for each of the meshes, 5 ch to turn, if the first mesh is an open one, 3 ch if it is solid. Then make 4 d c[1] for each solid mesh that stands alone, 7 d c for two meshes, etc.; the rule being 3 d c for each solid mesh and one additional d c every group of meshes. The number of d c is, in that case, always a multiple of 3, plus 1, as 4, 7, 10, 13, 16, 19, etc. For every open mesh make 2 ch and 1 d c in the top of d c below. The following designs are simple to work and very effective. **O** signifies open mesh, and **S,** solid mesh throughout.

Barbour's No. 40 F.D.A. Linen Crochet Thread would be suitable for working these patterns, or 30 if a coarser mesh is required.

The Cow.

1st Row.—84 ch, 14 squares of 4 tr, alternated with 13 open spaces of 3 ch.

2nd Row.—27 o.

3rd Row.—4 tr, 25 0, 4 tr.

4th Row.—5 o, 1 s, 11 o, 1 s, 9 o.

5th Row.—4 tr, 4 o, 1 s, 4 o, 1 s, 3 o, 1 s, 7 o, 1 s, 3 o, 4 tr.

6th Row.—4 o, 1 s, 6 o, 1 s, 4 o, 1 s, 3 o, 1 s, 6 o.

7th Row.—4 tr, 6 o, 1 s, 2 o, 1 s, 4 o, 1 s, 6 o, 1 s, 3 o, 4 tr.

8th Row.—4 o, 1 s, 2 o, 1 s, 1 o, 1 s, 1 o, 1 s, 4 o, 1 s, 1 o, 1 s, 8 o.

9th Row.—4 tr, 7 o, 4 s, 3 o, 1 s, 1 o, 3 s, 1 o, 2 s, 3 o, 4 tr.

10th Row.—4 o, 15 s, 8 o.

11th Row.—4 tr, 6 o, 15 s, 4 o, 4 tr.

12th Row.—5 o, 15 s, 7 o.

13th Row.—4 tr, 6 o, 16 s, 3 o, 4 tr.

14th Row.—4 o, 18 s, 5 o.

15th Row.—4 tr, 3 o, 3 s, 1 o, 15 s, 3 o, 4 tr.

16th Row.—3 o, 16 s, 2 o, 5 s, 3 o.

17th Row.—4 tr, 4 o, 19 s, 2 o, 4 tr.

18th Row.—4 o, 7 s, 5 o, 4 s, 1 o, 3 s, 3 o.

19th Row.—4 tr, 3 o, 6 s, 5 o, 1 s, 10 o, 4 tr.

20th Row.—12 o, 1 s, 4 o, 1 s, 2 o, 1 s, 6 o.

21st Row.—4 tr, 4 o, 1 s, 2 o, 1 s, 3 o, 2 s, 12 o, 4 tr.

22nd Row.—27 o.

23rd Row.—4 tr, 25 o, 4 tr.

24th Row.—27 o.

25th Row.—Same as 1st row.

[1] In this paragraph only, the term "d c" refers to the same stitch known as "d c" in modern American terminology.

Filet Mesh Crochet.

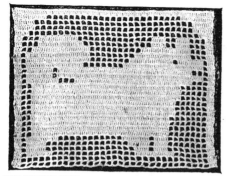

THE ESKIMO DOG.

The Eskimo Dog.

1st Row.—100 ch, 4 tr, 31 o, 4 tr.

2nd Row.—Same as 1st row.

3rd Row.—4 tr, 1 o, 4 s, 14 o, 6 s, 6 o, 4 tr.

4th Row.—4 tr, 7 o, 2 s, 1 o, 2 s, 15 o, 3 s, 1 o, 4 tr.

5th Row.—4 tr, 1 o, 3 s, 14 o, 3 s, 1 o, 2 s, 7 o, 4 tr.

6th Row.—4 tr, 7 o, 2 s, 1 o, 4 s, 11 o, 5 s, 1 o, 4 tr.

7th Row.—4 tr, 2 o, 22 s, 7 o, 4 tr.

8th Row.—4 tr, 7 o, 22 s, 2 o, 4 tr.

9th and 10th Rows.—Same as 8th row.

11th Row.—4 tr, 2 o, 23 s, 6 o, 4 tr.

12th and 13th Rows.—Same as 11th row.

14th, 15th and 16th Rows.—Same as 3 last, with 1 more s, and 1 less o.

17th Row.—4 tr, 1 o, 5 s, 3 o, 19 s, 3 o, 4 tr.

18th Row.—4 tr, 1 o, 24 s, 1 o, 4 s, 1 o, 4 tr.

19th Row.—4 tr, 1 o, 4 s, 1 o, 22 s, 3 o, 4 tr.

20th Row.—4 tr, 1 o, 13 s, 7 o, 9 s, 1 o, 4 tr.

21st Row.—4 tr, 1 o, 10 s, 7 o, 7 s, 1 o, 4 s, 1 o, 4 tr.

22nd Row.—4 tr, 3 o, 9 s, 8 o, 10 s, 1 o, 4 tr.

23rd Row.—4 tr, 2 o, 9 s, 9 o, 8 s, 3 o, 4 tr.

24th Row.—4 tr, 3 o, 2 s, 2 o, 2 s, 12 o, 7 s, 3 o, 4 tr.

25th Row.—4 tr, 3 o, 6 s, 13 o, 2 s, 2 o, 2 s, 3 o, 4 tr.

26th Row.—2 s, 29 o, 2 s.

27th Row.—3 s, 27 o, 3 s.

28th Row.—3 s, 27 o, 3 s.

29th Row.—5 s, 23 o, 5 s.

30th and last Row.—All treble.

The Swan.

1st Row.—106 ch, turn with 3 and make 10 tr, 2 o sp, 5 s, 5 o, 5 s, 5 o, 5 s, 2 o, 3 s.

2nd Row.—Turn with 3 ch, make 4 tr, 33 o, 4 tr.

3rd Row.—4 tr, 1 o, 4 s, 3 o, 4 s, 9 o, 4 s, 3 o, 4 s, 1 o, 4 tr.

4th Row.—Turn with 6 ch, 7 o, 1 s, 19 o, 1 s, 7 o.

5th Row.—6 o, 3 s, 8 o, 1 s, 8 o, 3 s, 6 o.

6th Row.—5 o, 1 s, 1 o, 1 s, 1 o, 1 s, 4 o, 3 s, 8 o, 1 s, 1 o, 1 s, 1 o, 1 s, 5 o.

7th Row.—20 o, 1 s, 14 o.

8th Row.—11 o, 13 s, 11 o.

9th Row.—10 o, 5 s, 3 o, 7 s, 10 o.

10th Row.—9 o, 11 s, 1 o, 5 s, 9 o.

11th Row.—8 o, 5 s, 1 o, 12 s, 9 o.

12th Row.—9 o, 13 s, 1 o, 3 s, 9 o.

13th Row.—12 o, 11 s, 1 o, 2 s, 9 o.

14th Row.—9 o, 2 s, 2 o, 11 s, 11 o.

15th Row.—12 o, 9 s, 3 o, 1 s, 10 o.

16th Row.—10 o, 2 s, 3 o, 7 s, 13 o.

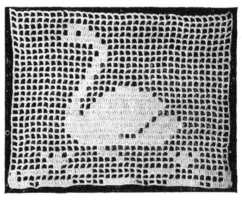

THE SWAN.

17th Row.—15 o, 3 s, 5 o, 1 s, 11 o.

18th Row.—11 o, 2 s, 22 o.

19th Row.—22 o, 1 s, 12 o.

20th Row.—12 o, 2 s, 21 o.

21st Row.—21 o, 1 s, 13 o.

22nd Row.—13 o, 2 s, 20 o.

23rd Row.—20 o, 1 s, 14 o.

24th Row.—13 o, 2 s, 20 o.

25th Row.—21 o, 6 s, 8 o.

26th Row.—9 o, 1 s, 1 o, 2 s, 22 o.

27th Row.—23 o, 3 s, 9 o.

28th and 29th Rows.—35 o sp.

The Boat.

1st Row.—93 ch, 3 s, 25 o, 3 s.

2nd Row.—1 s, 29 o, 1 s.

3rd Row.—1 s, 10 o, 16 s, 3 o, 1 s.

4th Row.—2 o, 19 s, 10 o.

5th Row.—2 o, 8 s, 6 o, 1 s, 14 o.

6th Row.—5 o, 10 s, 1 o, 3 s, 12 o.

7th Row.—3 o, 8 s, 1 o, 3 s, 1 o, 10 s, 5 o.

8th Row.—5 o, 10 s, 1 o, 2 s, 2 o, 6 s, 5 o.

9th Row.—7 o, 5 s, 1 o, 2 s, 1 o, 9 s, 6 o.

10th Row.—6 o, 9 s, 1 o, 2 s, 1 o, 4 s, 8 o.

11th Row.—14 o, 1 s, 1 o, 8 s, 7 o.

12th Row.—7 o, 8 s, 1 o, 1 s, 2 o, 5 s, 7 o.

13th Row.—7 o, 5 s, 2 o, 1 s, 1 o, 8 s, 7 o.

14th Row.—8 o, 7 s, 1 o, 1 s, 1 o, 5 s, 8 o.

15th Row.—8 o, 5 s, 1 o, 1 s, 1 o, 7 s, 8 o.

16th Row.—8 o, 7 s, 3 o, 4 s, 9 o.

17th Row.—9 o, 5 s, 2 o, 1 s, 2 o, 4 s, 8 o.

18th Row.—9 o, 3 s, 2 o, 1 s, 2 o, 3 s, 11 o.

19th Row.—11 o, 3 s, 2 o, 1 s, 2 o, 3 s, 9 o.

20th Row.—9 o, 2 s, 2 o, 2 s, 2 o, 2 s, 12 o.

21st Row.—12 o, 3 s, 1 o, 2 s, 3 o, 1 s, 9 o.

22nd Row.—9 o, 1 s, 2 o, 3 s, 1 o, 2 s, 13 o.

23rd Row.—13 o, 2 s, 1 o, 4 s, 11 o.

24th Row.—10 o, 5 s, 1 o, 1 s, 14 o.

25th Row.—14 o, 1 s, 1 o, 6 s, 9 o.

26th Row.—10 o, 5 s, 16 o.

27th Row.—16 o, 4 s, 11 o.

28th Row.—4 tr, 11 o, 3 s, 15 o, 4 tr.

29th Row.—7 tr, 14 o, 2 s, 11 o, 7 tr.

30th Row.—10 tr, 11 o, 1 s, 13 o. 10 tr.

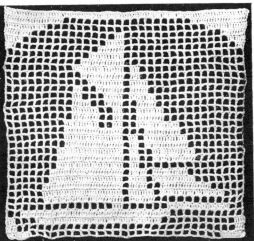

THE BOAT.

31st Row.—16 tr, 21 o, 16 tr.

32nd Row.—22 tr, 17 o, 22 tr.

33rd Row.—All tr.

The Windmill.

1st Row.—91 tr on 91 ch.

2nd Row.—Turn with 6 ch, 1 o, 1 s, 1 o, 1 s, 1 o, 1 s, 1 o, 1 s, 1 o, 12 s. Again 4 s with 1 o between each.

3rd Row.—7 o, 1 s, 3 o, 8 s, 3 o, 1s, 7 o.

4th Row.—7 o, 1 s, 3 o, 8 s, 3 o, 1 s, 7 o.

5th Row.—Same as last 2 rows.

6th Row.—6 o, 18 s. 6 o.

Filet Mesh Crochet.

7th Row.—7 o, 1 s, 3 o, 8 s, 3 o, 1 s, 7 o.

8th Row.—12 o, 6 s, 12 o.

9th Row.—6 o, 1 s, 5 o, 6 s, 5 o. 1 s, 6 o.

10th *Row.*—5 o, 3 s, 4 o, 6 s, 4 o, 3 s, 5 o.

11*th Row.*—4 o, 5 s, 3 o, 6 s. 3 o, 5 s, 4 o.

12*th Row.*—5 o, 5 s, 2 o, 6 s, 2 o, 5 s, 5 o.

13*th Row.*—6 o, 5 s, 1 o, 6 s, 1 o, 5 s, 5 o.

14*th Row.*—7 o, 4 s, 1 o, 6 s, 1 o, 4 s, 7 o.

15*th Row.*—8 o, 3 s, 1 o, 6 s, 1 o, 3 s, 8 o.

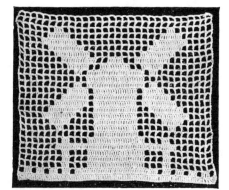

THE WINDMILL.

16*th Row.*—9 o, 1 s, 1 o, 8 s, 1 o, 1 s, 9 o.

17*th Row.*—11 o, 8 s, 11 o.

18*th Row.*—9 o, 1 s, 1 o, 8 s, 1 o, 1 s, 9 o.

19*th Row.*—8 o, 3 s, 2 o, 4 s, 2 o, 3 s, 8 o.

20*th Row.*—7 o, 5 s, 2 o, 2 s, 2 o, 5 s, 7 o.

21*st Row.*—6 o, 5 s, 8 o, 5 s, 6 o.

22*nd Row.*—5 o, 5 s, 10 o, 5 s, 5 o.

23*rd Row.*—4 o, 5 s, 12 o, 5 s, 4 o.

24*th Row.*—5 o, 3 s, 14 o, 3 s, 5 o.

25*th Row.*—6 o, 1 s, 16 o, 1 s, 6 o.

26*th* and 27*th Rows.*—30 o sp only.

The Cock.

1st Row.—53 o sp upon a ch.

2nd Row.—Same as 1st Row.

3rd Row.—34 o, 1 s, 1 o, 1 s, 1 o, 2 s, 13 o.

4th Row.—9 o, 1 s. 4 o, 4 s, 35 o.

5th Row.—35 o, 3 s, 3 o, 2 s, 10 o.

6th Row.—12 o, 1 s, 3 o, 1 s, 36 o.

7th Row.—36 o, 1 s, 2 o, 1 s, 13 o.

8th Row.—13 o, 2 s, 1 o, 1 s, 36 o.

9th Row.—36 o, 1 s, 2 o, 1 s, 13 o.

10*th Row.*—12 o, 3 s, 1 o, 1 s, 29 o, 1 s, 6 o.

11*th Row.*—6 o, 1 s, 20 o, 2 s, 5 o, 8 s, 11 o.

12*th Row.*—9 o, 9 s, 1 o, 2 s, 1 o, 6 s, 18 o, 2 s, 5 o.

13*th Row.*—4 o, 2 s, 1 o, 1 s, 3 o, 1 s, 3 o, 2 s, 2 o, 3 s, 2 o, 9 s, 1 o, 4 s, 1 o, 7 s, 7 o.

14*th Row.*—6 o, 8 s, 1 o, 5 s, 1 o, 8 s, 1 o, 8 s, 3 o, 1 s, 3 o, 1 s, 1 o, 2 s, 4 o.

15*th Row.*—4 o, 2 s, 1 o, 1 s, 2 o, 3 s, 2 o, 8 s, 3 o, 5 s, 1 o, 1 s, 7 o, 8 s, 5 o.

16*th Row.*—4 o, 7 s, 2 o, 6 s, 9 o, 9 s, 1 o, 1 s, 1 o, 3 s, 2 o, 1 s, 1 o, 2 s, 1 o, 1 s, 2 o.

17*th Row.*—2 o, 1 s, 1 o, 2 s, 1 o, 1 s, 1 o, 4 s, 1 o, 1 s, 1 o, 12 s, 1 o, 2 s, 1 o, 10 s, 1 o, 6 s, 4 o.

18*th Row.*—3 o, 6 s, 1 o, 11 s, 1 o, 2 s, 1 o, 6 s, 1 o, 5 s, 1 o, 1 s, 1 o, 4 s, 1 o, 1 s, 1 o, 2 s, 1 o, 1 s, 2 o.

19*th Row.*—2 o, 6 s, 1 o, 3 s, 1 o, 2 s, 2 o, 4 s, 1 o, 6 s, 1 o, 2 s, 1 o, 12 s, 2 o, 4 s, 3 o.

20*th Row.*—3 o, 4 s, 1 o, 12 s, 1 o, 8 s, 1 o, 5 s, 2 o, 3 s, 1 o, 3 s, 2 o, 5 s, 2 o.

21*st Row.*—2 o, 5 s, 1 o, 3 s, 3 o, 3 s, 1 o, 2 s, 1 o, 2 s, 1 o, 22 s, 1 o, 3 s, 3 o.

22*nd Row.*—3 o, 2 s, 1 o, 25 s, 1 o, 2 s, 1 o, 3 s, 2 o, 1 s, 1 o, 3 s, 1 o, 5 s, 2 o.

23*rd Row.*—2 o, 5 s, 1 o, 3 s, 1 o, 2 s, 2 o, 3 s, 2 o, 21 s, 1 o, 5 s, 1 o, 1 s, 3 o.

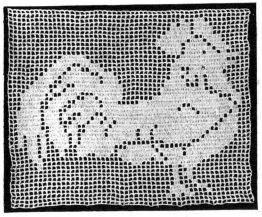

THE COCK·

Cock and Stag Designs.

39*th Row.*—34 o, 4 s, 1 o, 6 s, 1 o, 3 s, 4 o.

40*th Row.*—5 o, 3 s, 1 o, 5 s, 1 o, 5 s, 33 o.

41*st Row.*—33 o, 6 s, 1 o, 3 s, 1 o, 3 s, 6 o.

42*nd Row.*—6 o, 4 s, 2 o, 7 s, 34 o.

43*rd Row.*—35 o, 5 s, 1 o, 4 s, 8 o.

44*th Row.*—8 o, 4 s, 1 o, 4 s, 36 o.

45*th Row.*—36 o, 1 s, 1 o, 2 s, 1 o, 3 s, 9 o.

46*th Row.*—10 o, 2 s, 2 o, 1 s, 38 o.

47*th* and 48*th Rows.*—Same as 1st row.

The Stag.

1*st Row.*—142 ch, 4 s, 1 o, 2 s, alternated with 1 o 13 times, end with 3 s.

2*nd Row.*— 1 s, 45 o, 1 s.

3*rd Row.*—1 s, 3 o, 1 s, 2 o, 1 s, 31 o, 1 s, 6 o, 1 s.

4*th Row.*—1 s, 7 o, 1 s, 31 o, 1 s, 2 o, 1 s, 2 o, 1 s.

5*th Row.*—1 s, 3 o, 1 s, 2 o, 1 s, 29 o, 1 s, 4 o, 1 s, 3 o, 1 s.

6*th Row.*—1 s, 4 o, 1 s, 4 o, 1 s, 27 o, 1 s, 2 o, 1 s, 4 o, 1 s.

24*th Row.*—3 o, 8 s, 1 o, 2 s, 1 o, 25 s, 2 o, 3 s, 1 o, 5 s, 2 o.

25*th Row.*—3 o, 4 s, 2 o, 3 s, 2 o, 6 s, 1 o, 18 s, 2 o, 8 s, 1 o, 1 s, 2 o.

26*th Row.*—2 o, 2 s, 1 o, 19 s, 5 o, 3 s, 1 o, 5 s, 2 o, 4 s, 2 o, 4 s, 3 o.

27*th Row.*—3 o, 5 s, 2 o, 5 s, 2 o, 2 s, 1 o, 5 s, 7 o, 14 s, 3 o, 2 s, 2 o.

28*th Row.*—3 o, 3 s, 3 o, 10 s, 9 o, 6 s, 3 o, 4 s, 2 o, 1 s, 1 o, 5 s, 3 o.

29*th Row.*—4 o, 5 s, 1 o, 2 s, 1 o, 12 s, 9 o, 9 s, 2 o, 4 s, 4 o.

30*th Row.*—4 o, 5 s, 1 o, 1 s, 3 o, 4 s, 10 o, 10 s, 2 o, 2 s, 2 o, 4 s, 5 o.

31*st Row.*—6 o, 4 s, 2 o, 8 s, 1 o, 3 s, 11 o, 4 s, 1 o, 1 s, 1 o, 1 s, 1 o, 4 s, 5 o.

32*nd Row.*—5 o, 4 s, 1 o, 1 s, 1 o, 2 s, 1 o, 2 s, 12 o, 3 s, 1 o, 8 s, 1 o, 4 s, 7 o.

33*rd Row.*—8 o, 4 s, 1 o, 5 s, 2 o, 3 s, 13 o, 3 s, 1 o, 7 s, 6 o.

34*th Row.*—5 o, 8 s, 2 o, 2 s, 14 o, 4 s, 2 o, 2 s, 1 o, 4 s, 9 o.

35*th Row.*—11 o, 4 s, 2 o, 4 s, 16 o, 13 s, 3 o.

36*th Row.*—5 o, 11 s, 19 o, 7 s, 11 o.

37*th Row.*—12 o, 5 s, 21 o, 13 s, 2 o.

38*th Row.*—5 o, 1 s, 1 o, 2 s, 1 o 4 s, 1 o, 3 s, 35 o.

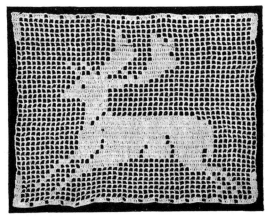

THE STAG·

93

Filet Mesh
Crochet.

7th Row.—1 s, 5 o, 1 s, 2 o, 1 s, 24 o, 2 s, 4 o, 1 s, 5 o, 1 s.

8th Row.—7 o, 1 s, 4 o, 3 s, 19 o, 6 s, 7 o.

9th Row.—10 o, 4 s, 13 o, 7 s, 4 o, 1 s, 8 o.

10th Row.—9 o, 2 s, 4 o, 7 s, 10 o, 4 s, 11 o.

11th Row.—9 o, 1 s, 1 o, 5 s, 1 o, 5 s, 1 o, 8 s, 1 o, 4 s, 11 o.

12th Row.—12 o, 4 s, 1 o, 7 s, 1 o, 5 s, 1 o, 5 s, 1 o, 1 s, 9 o.

13th Row.—9 o, 7 s, 1 o, 4 s, 1 o, 7 s, 1 o, 4 s, 13 o.

14th Row.—13 o, 4 s, 1 o, 11 s, 1 o, 8 s, 9 o.

15th Row.—9 o, 8 s, 1 o, 16 s, 13 o.

16th Row.—13 o, 16 s, 1 o, 8 s, 9 o.

17th Row.—9 o, 24 s, 14 o.

18th Row.—14 o, 1 s, 1 o, 21 s, 10 o.

19th Row.—12 o, 18 s, 1 o, 2 s, 14 o.

20th Row.—14 o, 3 s, 1 o, 1 s, 28 o.

21st Row.—29 o, 4 s, 14 o.

22nd Row.—14 o, 4 s, 29 o.

23rd Row.—29 o, 5 s, 13 o.

24th Row.—9 o, 9 s, 29 o.

25th Row.—29 o, 8 s, 10 o.

26th Row.—11 o, 2 s, 1 o, 7 s, 26 o.

27th Row.—21 o, 14 s, 12 o.

28th Row.—13 o, 5 s, 4 o, 1 s, 1 o, 4 s, 19 o.

29th Row.—18 o, 4s, 3 o, 1s, 1 o, 3 s, 1 o, 1 s, 2 o, 1 s, 12 o.

30th Row.—11 o, 1 s, 2 o, 1 s, 2 o, 4 s, 5 o, 5 s, 16 o.

31st Row.—15 o, 6 s, 4 o, 4 s, 4 o, 1 s, 2 o, 1 s, 10 o.

THE FUSCHIAS.

32nd Row.—19 o, 4 s, 4 o, 4 s, 16 o.

33rd Row.—17 o, 3 s, 3 o, 5 s, 19 o.

34th Row.—20 o, 3 s, 4 o, 4 s, 16 o.

35th Row.—16 o, 4 s, 4 o, 3 s, 20 o.

36th Row.—1 s, 19 o, 2 s, 5 o, 2 s, 1 o, 1 s, 15 o, 1 s.

37th Row.—1 s, 18 o, 1 s, 6 o, 1 s, 19 o, 1 s.

38th Row.—1 s, 19 o, 1 s, 25 o, 1 s.

39th Row.—1 s, 45 o, 1 s.

40th Row.—Same as 39th row.

41st Row.—4 s, 1 o, 2 s, alternated with 1 o 13 times, 3 s.

The Fuschias.

1st Row.—130 ch, 43 o.

2nd Row.—43 o.

3rd Row.—11 o, 2 s, 18 o, 2 s, 10 o.

4th Row.—10 o, 2 s, 18 o, 2 s, 11 o.

5th Row.—11 o, 1 s, 19 o, 1 s, 11 o.

6th Row.—8 o, 2 s, 1 o, 1 s, 1 o, 2 s, 13 o, 2 s, 1 o, 1 s, 1 o, 2 s, 8 o.

7th Row.—9 o, 1 s, 1 o, 1 s, 1 o, 1 s, 15 o, 1 s, 1 o, 1 s, 1 o, 1 s, 9 o.

8th, 9th and *10th Rows.*—S over s each time.

11th Row.—2 o, 1 s, 6 o, 1 s, 1 o, 1 s, 1 o, 1 s, 6 o, 1 s, 1 o, 1 s, 6 o, 1 s, 1 o, 1 s, 1 o, 1 s, 6 o, 1 s, 2 o.

12th Row.—3 o, 1 s, 3 o, 4 s, 1 o, 4 s, 3 o, 1 s, 3 o, 1 s, 3 o, 4 s, 1 o, 4 s, 3 o, 1 s, 3 o.

13th Row.—3 o, 2 s, 2 o, 9 s, 2 o, 2 s, 3 o, 2 s, 2 o, 9 s, 2 o, 2 s, 3 o.

14*th Row.*—
4 o, 2 s, 1 o, 9 s,
1 o, 2 s, 5 o, 2 s,
1 o, 9 s, 1 o, 2 s,
4 o.

15*th Row.*—
4 o, 3 s, 1 o, 7 s,
1 o, 3 s, 5 o, 3 s,
1 o, 7 s, 1 o, 3 s,
4 o.

16*th Row.*—
5 o, 3 s, 1 o, 5 s,
1 o, 3 s, 7 o, 3 s,
1 o, 5 s, 1 o, 3 s, 5 o.

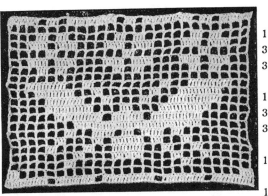

THE BUTTERFLY.

17*th Row.*—5 o, 4 s, 1 o, 3 s, 1 o, 4 s, 7 o, 4 s, 1 o, 3 s, 1 o, 4 s, 5 o.

18*th Row.*—6 o, 4 s, 1 o, 1 s, 1 o, 4 s, 9 o, 4 s, 1 o, 1 s, 1 o, 4 s, 6 o.

19*th Row.*—6 o, 5 s, 1 o, 5 s, 9 o, 5 s, 1 o, 5 s, 6 o.

20*th Row.*—7 o, 4 s, 1 o, 4 s, 11 o, 4 s, 1 o, 4 s, 7 o.

21*st Row.*—7 o, 4 s, 1 o, 4 s, 11 o, 4 s, 1 o, 4 s, 7 o.

22*nd Row.*—9 o, 2 s, 1 o, 2 s, 7 o, 1 s, 7 o, 2 s, 1 o, 2 s, 9 o.

23*rd Row.*—9 o, 2 s, 1 o, 2 s, 6 o, 3 s, 6 o, 2 s, 1 o, 2 s, 9 o.

24*th Row.*—10 o, 3 s, 6 o, 5 s, 6 o, 3 s, 10 o.

25*th,* 26*th,* 27*th,* 28*th* and 29*th Rows.*—Same as 24th row.

30*th Row.*—10 o, 3 s, 7 o, 3 s, 7 o, 3 s, 10 o.

31*st Row.*—Same as 30th row.

32*nd Row.*—10 o, 3 s, 8 o, 1 s, 8 o, 3 s, 10 o.

33*rd,* 34*th* and 35*th Rows.*—Same as 32nd row.

36*th Row.*—1 s, 10 o, 1 s, 9 o, 1 s, 9 o, 1 s, 10 o, 1 s.

37*th Row.*—1 s, 10 o, 1 s, 9 o, 1 s, 9 o, 1 s, 10 o, 1 s.

38*th Row.*—1 s, 7 o, 3 s, 1 o, 3 s, 6 o, 1 s, 6 o, 3 s, 1 o, 3 s, 7 o, 1 s.

39*th Row.*—
1 s, 4 o, 3 s, 7 o,
3 s, 7 o, 3 s, 7 o,
3 s, 4 o, 1 s.

40*th Row.*—
1 s, 1 o, 3 s, 13 o,
3 s, 1 o, 3 s, 13 o,
3 s, 1 o, 1 s.

41*st Row.*—
1 s, 41 o, 1 s.

42*nd Row.*—
1 s, 10 o, 1 s, 9 o
1 s, 9 o, 1 s, 10 o,
1 s.

43*rd Row.*—4 s, 4 o, 7 s, 4 o, 5 s, 4 o, 7 s, 4 o, 4 s.

The Butterfly.

1*st Row.*—76 ch, 4 s, 1 o, 4 s, 1 o, 5 s, 1 o, 4 s, 1 o, 4 s.

2*nd Row.*—1 s, 23 o, 1 s.

3*rd Row.*—6 o, 1 s, 11 o, 1 s, 6 o.

4*th Row.*—7 o, 1 s, 3 o, 3 s, 3 o, 1 s, 2 o, 1 s, 4 o.

5*th Row.*—5 o, 1 s, 2 o, 1 s, 2 o, 3 s, 2 o, 1 s, 3 o, 1 s, 4 o.

6*th Row.*—5 o, 1 s, 3 o, 1 s, 1 o, 3 s, 1 o, 1 s, 2 o, 1 s, 6 o.

7*th Row.*—7 o, 1 s, 1 o, 2 s, 1 o, 1 s, 1 o, 2 s, 2 o, 1 s, 6 o.

8*th Row.*—7 o, 13 s, 5 o.

9*th Row.*—5 o, 5 s, 1 o, 3 s, 1 o, 5 s, 5 o.

10*th Row.*—4 o, 5 s, 3 o, 1 s, 3 o, 5 s, 4 o.

11*th Row.*—3 o, 5 s, 2 o, 1 s, 3 o, 1 s, 2 o, 4 s, 4 o.

12*th Row.*—3 o, 4 s, 2 o, 1 s, 5 o, 1 s, 2 o, 4 s, 3 o.

13*th Row.*—2 o, 4 s, 2 o, 1 s, 7 o, 1 s, 2 o, 4 s, 2 o.

14*th Row.*—25 o only.

15*th Row.*—3 o, 1 s, 1 o, 1 s, 5 o, 1 s, 1 o, 1 s, 5 o, 1 s, 1 o, 1 s, 3 o.

16*th Row.*—2 o, 2 s, 1 o, 2 s, 3 o, 2 s, 1 o, 2 s, 3 o, 2 s, 1 o, 2 s, 2 o.

Filet Mesh Crochet.

17th Row.—4 o, 1 s, 7 o, 1 s, 7 o, 1 s, 4 o.

18th Row.—2 o, 2 s, 1 o, 2 s, 3 o, 2 s, 1 o, 2 s, 3 o, 2 s, 1 o, 2 s, 2 o.

19th Row.—3 o, 1 s, 1 o, 1 s, 5 o, 1 s, 1 o, 1 s, 5 o, 1 s, 1 o, 1 s, 3 o.

20th Row.—25 o only.

21st Row.—3 s, 1 o, 1 s, 1 o, 5 s, 1 o, 1 s, 1 o, 5 s, 1 o, 1 s, 1 o, 3 s.

The Stork.

1st Row.—94 ch. Turn with 4 tr. 1 o alternated with 2 s nine times, 1 s.

2nd Row.—2 s, 2 o, 1 s, 2 o, 1 s, 2 o, 1 s, 2 o, 1 s, 2 o, 1 s, 2 o, 1 s, 2 o, 1s. 2 o, 1 s, 2 o, 2 s.

3rd Row.—1 s, 28 o, 1 s.

4th Row.—1 s, 13 o, 2 s, 13 o, 1 s.

5th Row.—1 s, 14 o, 1 s, 13 o, 1 s.

6th Row.—1 s, 13 o, 1 s, 14 o, 1 s.

7th, 8th and 9th Rows.—S over s, o over o.

10th Row.—1 s, 12 o, 2 s, 14 o, 1 s.

11th Row.—1 s, 14 o, 1 s, 13 o, 1 s.

12th Row.—1 s, 3 o, 1 s, 9 o, 2 s, 2 o, 1 s, 10 o, 1 s.

13th Row.—1 s, 11 o, 6 s, 6 o, 3 s, 2 o, 1 s.

14th Row.—1 s, 2 o, 3 s, 5 o, 1 s, 1 o, 4 s, 12 o, 1 s.

15th Row.—1 s, 11 o, 6 s, 1 o, 1 s, 3 o, 4 s, 2 o, 1 s.

16th Row.—1 s, 2 o, 5 s, 1 o, 1 s, 1 o, 8 s, 10 o, 1 s.

17th Row.—1 s, 9 o, 17 s, 2 o, 1 s.

18th Row.—1 s, 3 o, 17 s, 8 o, 1 s.

19th Row.—1 s, 7 o, 16 s, 5 o, 1 s.

20th Row.—1 s, 7 o, 15 s, 6 o, 1 s.

21st Row.—1 s, 6 o, 3 s, 2 o, 8 s, 9 o, 1 s.

22nd Row.—1 s, 12 o, 3 s, 4 o, 2 s, 7 o, 1 s.

23rd Row.—1 s, 8 o, 2 s, 18 o, 1 s.

24th Row.—1 s, 18 o, 2 s, 5 o, 1 s, 2 o, 1 s.

25th Row.—1 s, 3 o, 1 s, 5 o, 2 s, 17 o, 1 s.

26th Row.—1 s, 16 o, 2 s, 5 o, 1s, 4 o, 1 s.

27th Row.—1 s, 5 o, 2 s, 4 o, 2 s, 15 o, 1s.

28th Row.—1 s, 15 o, 2 s, 1 o, 4 s, 6 o, 1 s.

29th Row.—1 s, 6 o, 2 s, 1 o, 4 s, 15 o, 1 s.

30th Row.—2 s, 15 o, 5 s, 6 o, 2 s.

31st Row.—3 s, 24 o, 3 s.

32nd Row.—4 s, 22 o, 4 s.

33rd Row.—Treble the whole length of the row.

The Runaway Chicken.

1st Row.—70 ch, turn with 3 and make 2 s, alternated with 1 o seven times, 2 s.

2nd Row.—1 s, 21 o, 1 s.

3rd Row.—23 o.

4th Row.—Same as 2nd row.

5th Row.—1 s, 10 o, 1 s, 10 o. 1 s.

6th Row.—11 o, 2 s, 10 o.

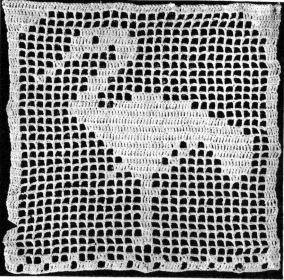

THE STORK.

96

7th Row.—1s, 11 o, 1 s, 5 o, 1 s, 3 o, 1 s.

8th Row.—1 s, 2 o, 2 s. 4 o, 1 s, 12 o, 1 s.

9th Row.—9 o, 6 s, 2 o, 1 s, 5 o.

10th Row.—1 s, 5 o, 9 s, 7 o, 1 s.

11th Row.—1 s, 5 o, 9 s, 7 o, 1 s.

12th Row.—7 o, 2 s, 2 o, 6 s, 6 o.

13th Row.—1 s, 5 o, 8 s, 1 o, 2 s, 5 o, 1 s.

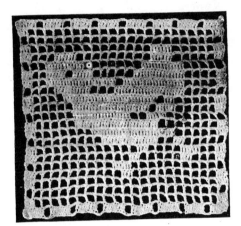

THE RUNAWAY CHICKEN.

14th Row.—1 s, 5 o, 1 s, 1 o, 10 s, 4 o, 1 s.

15th Row.—4 o, 4 s, 3 o, 7 s, 5 o.

16th Row.—1 s, 4 o, 6 s, 1 o, 8 s, 2 o, 1 s.

17th Row.—1 s, 2 o, 2 s, 1 o, 2 s, 5 o, 5 s, 4 o, 1 s.

18th Row.—5 o, 4 s, 7 o, 4 s, 3 o.

19th Row.—1 s, 3 o, 2 s, 9 o, 2 s, 5 o. 1 s.

20th Row.—1 s, 5 o, 2 s, 14 o, 1 s.

21st Row.—23 o.

22nd Row.—1 s, 21 o, 1 s.

23rd Row.—Same as 1st row.

"Dandy."

1st Row.—72 ch, 2 s, 1 o, 2 s, 1 o, 2 s, 1 o, 2 s, 1 o, 2 s, 1 o, 2 s, 1 o. 3 s.

2nd Row.—1 s, 22 o, 1 s.

3rd Row.—1 s, 2 o, 1 s, 3 o, 2 s. 1 o, 1 s, 2 o, 1 s, 1 o, 1 s, 1 o, 1 s, 2 o, 2 s, 1 o, 1 s.

4th Row.—2 o, 1 s, 1 o, 1 s, 1 o, 3 s, 1 o, 1 s, 1 o, 2 s, 1 o, 1 s, 1 o, 1 s, 2 o, 1 s, 2 o, 1 s.

5th Row.—1 s, 1 o, 1 s, 1 o, 1 s, 1 o, 1 s, 1 o, 1 s, 1 o, 1 s, 1 o, 2 s, 1 o, 1 s, 1 o, 1 s, 1 o, 1 s, 1 o, 1 s, 1 o, 1 s.

6th Row.—1 s, 1 o, 2 s, 3 o, 2 s, 1 o, 1 s, 2 o, 1 s, 1 o, 2 s, 2 o, 1 s, 1 o, 1 s, 1 o, 1 s.

7th Row.—1 s, 23 o.

8th Row.—1 s, 4 o, 2 s, 10 o, 2 s, 4 o, 1 s.

9th Row.—1 s, 4 o, 1 s, 10 o, 2 s, 5 o, 1 s.

10th Row.—6 o, 3 s, 1 o, 4 s, 2 o, 3 s, 4 o, 1 s.

11th Row.—1 s, 3 o, 10 s, 1 o, 3 s, 5 o, 1 s.

12th Row.—1 s, 4 o, 15 s, 3 o, 1 s.

13th Row.—1 s, 2 o, 17 s, 4 o.

14th Row.—1 s, 3 o, 17 s, 2 o, 1 s.

15th Row.—1 s, 2 o, 17 s, 3 o, 1 s.

"DANDY."

16th Row.—5 o, 10 s, 3 o, 3 s, 2 o, 1 s.

17th Row.—1 s, 2 o, 2 s, 1 o, 13 s, 4 o, 1 s.

18th Row.—1 s, 3 o, 16 s, 3 o, 1 s.

19th Row.—1 s, 3 o, 7 s, 3 o, 7 s, 3 o.

Filet Mesh Crochet.

20th Row.—1 s, 2 o, 2 s, 1 o,
4 s, 4 o, 6 s, 3 o, 1 s.

21st Row.—1 s, 4 o, 4 s, 6 o,
5 s, 3 o, 1 s.

22nd Row.—5 o, 1 s, 1 o, 1 s,
15 o. 1 s.

23rd Row.—1 s, 22 o, 1 s.

24th Row—Same as 23rd row.

25th Row.—2 s, alternated
with 1 o seven times, 3 s.

The Squirrel.

1st Row.—82 ch, 27 o.

2nd and 3rd Rows.—Same as
1st row.

4th Row.—3 o, 9 s, 2 o, 6 s,
7 o.

5th Row.—6 o, 8 s, 1 o, 1 s, 11 o.

6th Row.—10 o, 3 s, 1 o, 2 s, 2 o, 4 s,
5 o.

7th Row.—4 o, 4 s, 3 o, 1 s, 2 o, 4 s,
9 o.

8th Row.—8 o, 9 s, 3 o, 3 s, 4 o.

9th Row.—3 o, 4 s, 3 o, 10 s, 7 o.

10th Row.—7 o, 5 s, 1 o, 4 s, 3 o, 4 s,
3 o.

11th Row.—3 o, 4 s, 3 o, 5 s, 1 o, 3 s,
8 o.

12th Row.—11 o, 6 s, 3 o, 4 s, 3 o.

13th Row.—3 o, 5 s, 2 o, 7 s, 10 o.

14th Row.—3 o, 6 s, 1 o, 6 s, 3 o,
5 s, 3 o.

15th Row.—4 o, 5 s, 2 o, 5 s, 1 o, 3 s,
2 o, 1 s, 4 o.

16th Row.—7 o, 8 s, 3 o, 5 s, 4 o.

17th Row.—5 o, 5 s, 2 o, 8 s, 2 o,
1 s, 4 o.

18th Row.—4 o, 2 s, 1 o, 7 s, 2 o,,
6 s, 5 o.

19th Row.—6 o, 6 s, 2 o, 8 s, 1 o,
1 s, 3 o.

20th Row.—3 o, 8 s, 3 o, 7 s, 6 o.

21st Row.—7 o, 7 s, 4 o, 5 s, 4 o.

22nd Row.—5 o, 1 s, 1 o, 1 s, 5 o,
6 s, 8 o.

23rd Row.—8 o, 6 s, 13 o.

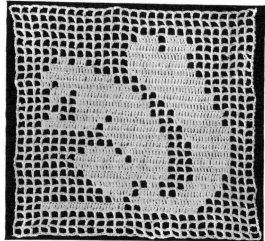

THE SQUIRREL.

24th Row.—13 o, 3 s, 1 o, 3 s, 7 o.

25th Row.—8 o, 2 s, 1 o, 2 s, 14 open.

26th, 27th and 28th Rows.—27 open
spaces.

The Goose and Gosling.

1st Row.—106 ch, 4 s, 2 o, 2 s, alternated with 2 o six times, 5 s.

2nd Row.—1 s, 33 o, 1 s.

3rd Row.—1 s, 7 o, 1 s, 3 o, 1 s, 8 o,
2 s, 1 o, 1 s, 9 o, 1 s.

4th Row.—1 s, 6 o, 1 s, 1 o, 1 s, 1 o,
1 s, 11 o, 1 s, 1 o, 1 s, 8 o, 1 s.

5th Row.—1 s, 6 o, 7 s, 9 o, 1 s, 2 o,
1 s, 7 o, 1 s.

6th Row.—1 s, 8 o, 1 s, 1 o, 1 s, 8 o,
9 s, 5 o, 1 s.

7th Row.—1 s, 4 o, 5 s, 2 o, 3 s, 7 o,
3 s, 9 o, 1 s.

8th Row.—1 s, 7 o, 6 s, 5 o, 3 s, 1 o,
8 s, 3 o, 1 s.

9th Row.—1 s, 2 o, 10 s, 1 o, 2 s, 4 o,
9 s, 5 o, 1 s.

10th Row.—5 o, 11 s, 3 o, 2 s, 1 o,
4 s, 1 o, 2 s, 1 o, 1 s, 4 o.

11th Row.—4 o, 3 s, 4 o, 1 s, 1 o, 3 s,
2 o, 5 s, 2 o, 7 s, 3 o.

12th Row.—1 s, 5 o, 6 s, 2 o, 4 s, 2 o,
1 s, 13 o, 1 s.

13th Row.—1 s, 16 o, 3 s, 1 o, 7 s, 6 o, 1 s.

14th Row.—8 o, 6 s, 1 o, 4 s, 16 o.

15th Row.—16 o, 3 s, 1 o, 6 s, 8 o, 1 s,

16th Row.—1 s, 9 o, 5 s, 1 o, 3 s, 15 o, 1 s.

17th Row.—1 s, 15 o, 8 s, 11 o.

18th Row.—12 o, 7 s, 16 o.

19th Row.—17 o, 4 s, 13 o, 1 s.

20th Row.—1 s, 14 o, 3 s, 16 o, 1 s,

21st Row.—1 s, 16 o, 3 s, 15 o.

22nd Row.—1 s, 14 o, 2 s, 18 o.

23rd Row.—18 o, 2 s, 14 o, 1 s.

24th Row.—15 o, 2 s, 17 o, 1 s.

25th Row.—1 s, 17 o, 2 s, 15 o.

26th Row.—1 s, 14 o, 2 s, 18 o.

27th Row.—1 s, 14 o, 5 s, 15 o.

28th Row.—1 s, 15 o, 1 s, 1 o, 1 s, 16 o.

29th Row.—1 s, 15 o, 3 s, 15 o, 1 s.

30th Row.—1 s, 33 o, 1 s.

31st Row.—Same as 30th row.

32nd Row.—5 s, 2 o, 2 s, alternated with 2 o six times, 4 s.

Dog and Cat with Ball.[1]

1st and *2nd Rows.*— 57 o.

3rd Row.—2 o, 7 s, 1 o, 5 s, 4 o, 2 s, 10 o, 7 s, 1 o, 5 s, 3 o, 2 s, 2 o, 2 s, 4 o.

4th Row.—4 o, 2 s, 1 o, 6 s, 2 o, 4 s, 6 o, 1 s, 11 o, 6 s, 2 o, 3 s, 5 o, 2 s, 2 o.

5th Row.—2 o, 11 s, 1 o, 4 s, 1 o, 1 s, 5 o, 2 s, 4 o, 12 s, 1 o, 2 s, 1 o, 1 s, 5 o, 2 s, 2 o.

6th Row.—2 o, 2 s, 5 o, 1 s, 1 o, 2 s, 1 o, 11 s. 5 o, 2 s, 5 o, 1 s, 1 o, 4 s, 1 o, 10 s, 3 o.

7th Row.—5 o, 8 s, 1 o, 3 s, 1 o, 2 s, 4 o, 2 s, 8 o, 9 s, 1 o, 1 s, 1 o, 2 s, 4 o, 2 s, 3 o.

8th Row.—4 o, 3 s, 1 o, 3 s, 1 o, 2 s, 1 o, 8 s, 9 o, 3 s, 1 o, 4 s, 1 o, 3 s, 1 o, 7 s, 5 o.

9th Row.—6 o, 5 s. 1 o, 10 s, 1 o, 1 s, 10 o, 7 s, 1 o, 8 s, 1 o, 1 s, 5 o.

10th Row.—7 o, 9 s, 1 o, 5 s, 13 o, 10 s, 2 o, 3 s, 7 o.

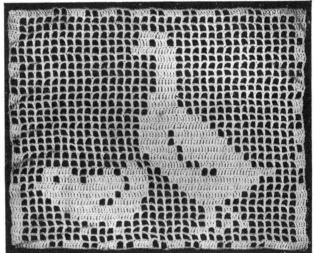

THE GOOSE AND GOSLING.

[1]The photograph on the next page shows the cat on the right moved one square to the right.

11th Row.
—8 o, 14 s,
13 o, 3 s,
2 o, 10 s,
7 o.

12th Row.
—7 o, 13 s,
14 o, 1 s,
2 o, 11 s,
9 o.

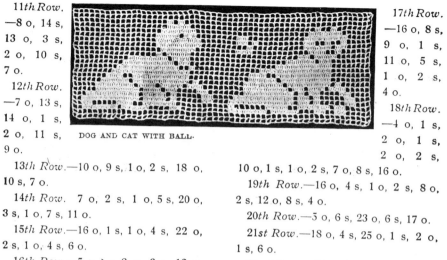

DOG AND CAT WITH BALL.

17th Row.
—16 o, 8 s,
9 o, 1 s,
11 o, 5 s,
1 o, 2 s,
4 o.

18th Row.
—4 o, 1 s,
2 o, 1 s,
2 o, 2 s,

13th Row.—10 o, 9 s, 1 o, 2 s, 18 o, 10 s, 7 o.

14th Row. 7 o, 2 s, 1 o, 5 s, 20 o, 3 s, 1 o, 7 s, 11 o.

15th Row.—16 o, 1 s, 1 o, 4 s, 22 o, 2 s, 1 o, 4 s, 6 o.

16th Row.—5 o, 1 s, 2 o, 3 s, 12 o, 3 s, 8 o, 6 s, 17 o.

10 o, 1 s, 1 o, 2 s, 7 o, 8 s, 16 o.

19th Row.—16 o, 4 s, 1 o, 2 s, 8 o, 2 s, 12 o, 8 s, 4 o.

20th Row.—5 o, 6 s, 23 o, 6 s, 17 o.

21st Row.—18 o, 4 s, 25 o, 1 s, 2 o, 1 s, 6 o.

22nd Row.—36 o, 1 s, 1 o, 1 s, 18 o.

23rd and 24th Rows.—57 o.

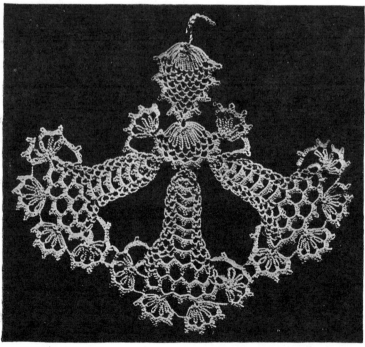

A CROCHETED SPRAY.

Directions for working this design appear on page 105.

Section VIII.

ODDMENTS IN CROCHET.

A Leaf Oddment for Appliqué.

Use Ardern's crochet cotton, No. 36, for this motif.

25 ch, 1 d c into each of first 19, catch up the first ch to form a ring, into which put 12 tr, turn, 3 ch, 1 tr into first tr, 2 ch, 1 tr into each tr, turn, 3 ch, 2 tr into each sp, turn, 3 ch, 1 tr into first tr, 2 ch, 1 tr into each of the next 5 trs, 2 ch, 1 tr into same tr as last, 7 ch, 1 d c into second next tr, 7 ch, 1 tr into second next tr, 2 ch, 1 tr into same tr as last, 2 ch, 1 tr into each of next 5 tr, 2 ch, 1 tr into same tr as last, 7 ch, 1 d c into second next tr, 7 ch, 1 tr into second next tr, 2 ch, 1 tr into same tr as last, 2 ch, 1 tr into each of next 5 tr, turn, into first sp, * 1 d c, 3 ch, 2 tr into next, 2 ch, 2 long tr into next, 2 ch, 2 long tr (thread over 3 times) into next twice, 2 ch, 2 long tr into next, 2 ch, 2 tr into next, 2 ch, 1 d c into next, 7 ch, 1 d c into next,

A LEAF ODDMENT FOR APPLIQUÉ.

7 ch, 1 d c into next, 7 ch, and repeat from * twice.

In the last row put 2 d c, 4 ch, 2 d c into each sp between the trs, but between the centre long trs put 3 d c at each side of the 4 ch, 4 d c over the 7 ch loop, 7 ch, 1 d c into next loop, 7 ch, 4 d c over end of next loop.

An Ornament for a Tie or Jabot.

Form 14 ch into a ring, 16 ch, 1 d c into the ring 9 times, turn, 8 d c up the side of last loop, 5 ch, 1 d c into the top of each loop, turn, * 2 ch, 1 d c into top of last loop, 5 ch, 1 d c into each loop *, repeat until only one loop remains, break off the thread and fasten again to the last of the 8 d c up the side, put into each sp all round, 2 d c, 4 ch, 2 d c, 8 d c down the side of last loop, 6 d c into the ring, 12 ch for the stem, 1 d c into each ch of

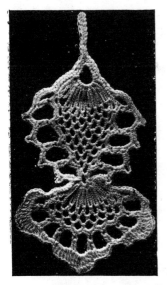

stem, 6 d c into ring, break off the thread.

Into the picot at the point put 9 loops of 16 ch each, and into the loops 5 ch, 1 d c each, work 3 rows of these loops, putting 7 ch at the turning, then slip stitch down to the top of long loop, turn, and put 2 d c, 4 ch, 2 d c into each sp all round. Turn, 5 ch, 2 tr into each picot all round, ending at the opposite side with 5 ch, 1 d c.

SUITABLE FOR AN INSET.

Work 5 ch, 2 tr into each picot at each side of the first leaf, then starting at the right side of the ring, put 1 d c into each all round the ring and stem, into the 8 d c at the side, and next sp; into each of next 4 sp 3 d c, 4 ch, 3 d c, 8 d c into side of long loop, * 6 tr into next sp, 2 tr into the 2 tr, 6 long tr into next, 2 tr into the 2 tr, 6 tr into next sp, 2 d c into the 2 tr, * repeat twice more, then finish next side to correspond with the last.

Suitable for an Inset in Linen or a Handkerchief Border.

Use Ardern's No. 40 Cotton. Make 28 ch, 1 d c in 20th, 10 loops of 18 ch in the little ring, 9 up the side of last one. Into each loop make 2 more loops of 18 ch each, with 5 ch between each 2.

9 ch to top of last loop, catch with 1 d c in each loop, two and two, meeting them over the 5 ch. Make 10 ch between each time.

so that there are 9 sp.

Fill each sp with 3 ordinary tr, 3 long tr, 5 ch, 3 long tr, 3 ordinary tr, 1 d c. When joined, lead down to the stem with ch from the last tr. Make a longer ch than the one there, d c in each ch till the other length is reached, then d c over the 2, catching in a ch now and then.

A Handkerchief Corner.

Use No. 80 Cotton. Cut the hem off a hemstitched handkerchief close against the stitches without cutting them. Press the hook through each stitch; if not open enough, a d c must go into each tiny hole; if they are very close together one or two must have a d c in them without the loops of ch.

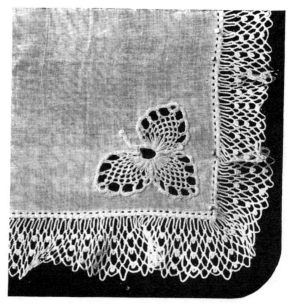

A HANDKERCHIEF CORNER.

A SMALL ODDMENT.

This pattern has 13 loops of 16 ch to the inch, which makes it the requisite fulness ; at the corner put 3 loops in 1 sp. Should the lace be required deeper than this one of 8 rows, extra loops should be made at the corner half way.

2nd Row.—Across to each loop 9 ch, 2 d c in each loop.

3rd Row.—In the 9 ch make 2 d c, 5 ch, 2 d c. 7 ch to next sp, 2 d c. 7 ch, and again 2 d c, 5 ch, 2 d c.

4th Row.—Into each sp 2 d c, with 9 ch between.

5th Row.—Same as 3rd.

6th Row.—Same as 4th.

To make a little difference in the last row, let the ch be 9 and 12, 2 d c in each sp.

The inset spray is closely sewn all round through the tops of the d c which surrounds it. Before cutting away the lawn at the back, if necessary for strength, again sew the raw edges at the back into the stitches.

A Small Oddment.

Use Strutt's No. 36, or Ardern's No. 40 Cotton. Ch 42, catch back into the 12th ch from hook, so as to form a ring. Into this ring make 14 loops of 18 ch each. Go up the side of last loop with 9 ch, catch the loops, 2 and 2, with a d c in each one. Ch 10, catch back into the 5th with a d c to

form a small loop, ch 5, and catch into next pair of long loops.

At the last loop, turn and fill in with 5 d c, 4 loops of 12 ch in the tiny loop, then another 5 d c.

From the last d c make a ch to go down to the stem. Make another length of ch, and d c over it into the one first made to give the necessary thickness.

An Ivy-Leaf in Open Crochet.

Use No. 40 Cotton. Ch 9, join in a ring, into this make 6 loops of 18 ch each. After making the 6th loop, ch 9 and catch into top of the 6th loop, ch 9, catch into top of 5th loop, ch 9, catch into 4th loop, ch 18, catch into 3rd loop, ch 9, catch into 2nd loop, ch 9, catch into the top of first loop made.

Turn and put 9 d c into each of the 9 ch in previous row, making a loop of 18 ch exactly over each loop in the previous row. On reaching the centre of the leaf, where you made 18 instead of 9 ch in the previous row, make 2 loops of 18 ch each in the centre instead of 1, with 9 d c each side. Study the illustration.

Now go up the side of the last loop

AN IVY-LEAF IN OPEN CROCHET.

in the row with 9 ch, and proceed as before, uniting the loops with 9 ch, only making 18 ch between the 2 centre loops.

When you have made 4 rows in all, do not turn round at the last loop and fill in with d c, but instead work down the lower side of the leaf toward the stem, with 9 ch and catching into the end of each row. On reaching the tiny ring, make 3 d c into it. Then ch 40 to form stem, and catch into the ring, ch 20, and catch into the bottom of the stem, making 3 strands in all. Make d c all up the stem again, over 2 strands, but change the strands each time. 3 d c into the other side of the little ring; then work all round the edge of the leaf to complete it with 9 d c in each space, and 6 ch to form the picot loop at the end of each row.

Three Crochet Motifs.

No. 1.—With No. 40 cotton make a ring of 36 ch, 3 ch, 11 tr into the ring, * 16 ch, 1 d c into the ring twice, 13 ch, 12 tr, repeat from * until there are 4 groups of tr and loops.

2nd Row.—Slipstitch across 2 tr, 1 tr into each of next 8, 7 ch, 1 d c into each loop all round, and 8 tr on the centre 8 of each group.

3rd, 4th and 5th Rows.—Repeat the 2nd, omitting the first and last tr in each group in each successive row and putting 9 ch in each loop.

After the last tr, form 80 ch and fasten to the tr, 40 ch, fasten to the

No. 2.　　　No. 3.　　　No. 1.
MOTIFS FOR APPLIQUÉ.

end of the doubled ch, and over this stem work d c closely.

No. 2 is worked in the same way as the preceding, but smaller. Commence on a ring of 24 ch, and put only 10 tr in each group, in the next row put 8, then 4 and finally 2, make the stem only half the length.

No. 3.—Make a ring of 20 ch, into the ring put 12 tr, 6 loops of 12 ch each, 12 tr, turn, 1 tr into each tr, 7 ch into each loop, tr into each tr, turn.

3rd and 4th Rows.—Repeat the 2nd, omitting the first and last tr.

5th Row.—8 tr into the 10, 8 tr into next sp, 1 d c into next sp, then a loop into each, and make the opposite side to correspond.

In each of the following 4 rows put a tr into each tr, and continue the 4th row into the next space as in the 5th. Then on the last 8 tr work 2 more rows, ending with 2 rows of tr into the top sp. Form the stem as in the preceding motifs.

A Crocheted Spray.

This design is illustrated on page 100.

It is worked in Barbour's 120 Linen Lace Thread. It would make a handsome edge if repeated round a tea-cloth, or it would do equally well if applied to a jabot or the ends of a net tie.

Ch 12 and join in a ring. Into this make 9 loops of 18 ch each. Ch 9 to carry you up the side of the last loop and then connect each loop with 5 ch in between. Turn at the end of the row, and make 5 ch into those in the previous row. Proceed to make the fine network of the cone in this way, each row being shorter than the previous row, till you have only 5 ch at the tip.

From this tip, work down the side of the cone to the stern part (the place you started from), putting into each alternate little space 3 d c, 6 ch. 3 d c; and fill the intervening little spaces with 3 d c. When you reach the last little space, ch 9 to carry you along the side of the loop and catch into ring first made. Then chain as much as seems required to form the stem, and return with a d c into each ch. This brings you back to the starting ring. Ch 9 and go up the opposite side of the loops, then work up this side of the cone as you did the other side, till you are back at the tip again.

From the tip of the cone a little fan is made, exactly as you made the first part of the cone, but only three rows of network are done (by making the 5 ch), and these rows are not decreased at each turn. Fill in all round the top of this fan with 3 d c, 6 ch, 3 d c into each little space.

Break off and work in the end of the cotton.

To make the trumpet-like flowers at the lower part of the spray: Into the 3rd tiny picot loop in the edge of the fan make 5 loops of 6 ch each. Turn, and make 6 ch into each of these loops.

Turn, into first loop 6 ch, into second loop 6 ch, into third loop 5 d c, 6 ch, 5 d c, into fourth loop 6 ch, into fifth loop 6 ch.

* Turn with 6 ch into first and second loop, 7 ch into third loop, 6 ch into fourth and fifth loop.

Turn, 6 ch into first and second loop; 5 d c, 6 ch, 5 d c into third loop; 6 ch into fourth and fifth loop. Repeat from * till there are seven bars in all up the centre of the pattern. On reaching the eighth bar, make a similar bar each side of it (*i.e.*, three in the row) by filling in the loop on either side with 5 d c, 6 ch, 5 d c.

The next time make 4 bars across, and, finally, make 6 bars across. Break off.

Into the little picot loop in the top of the first bar, make 5 loops of 12 ch each. Then 6 ch to carry you up the side of the last loop, catch in top of loop, connect each of the loops with 6 ch between. Then ch 10, and catch this into the side of the trumpet part of the flower (study the illustration). Return along this with 5 d c, 6 ch, 5 d c, over this 10 ch; then fill in each of the 6 ch, with 3 d c, 6 ch, 3 d c. From the last one ch 10, and go across into the third picot loop at the bottom of the flower, and make another little fan.

In this way the four fans at the bottom are made, and a bar of 10 ch is made on the opposite to catch into the trumpet-part of the flower, as has

A HONITON BRAID AND
CROCHET ODDMENT.

already been explained. Complete each flower in this way.

There are still two small fans to be made, one on either side, near the tip of the cone. These are made last of all, in just the same way as the fans at the lower side of the flower.

A Honiton Braid and Crochet Oddment.

Fine Honiton braid with an open lobe is required for this medallion.

Cut off 11 lobes of the braid. With Barbour's No. 90 Linen Lace Thread make a d c in the centre edge of the 1st lobe, form a long tr into the centre of the 2nd lobe, keep the last loop of this and the following trs on the hook, in each side of next lobe make a triple tr (thread three times over the needle) at the nearest side of next lobe make a quadruple tr (thread four times over the needle), work off the first loops of this tr, thread over the needle and into the other side of lobe, then work off the entire tr except

last loop, repeat the quadruple trs into next lobe, then triple trs into next, long tr into next, work off all the loops on the needle, 1 d c into next lobe centre, draw the 2 d c's close together with a single stitch, cross over to the outer edge of the braid with a triple tr and fasten the two edges of the lobes to form a circle. The remaining 3 lobes form a stem around which d c is worked closely into the edge and over the bars between the lobes.

For the outer rows, fasten the thread on the back of the stem at the 1st lobe, 4 ch, 3 d c into the centre of the lobe, 4 ch, 1 d c into the end of the lobe, 3 ch, 3 d c over the lobe, 3 ch, * 1 tr into the edge of the braid, 2 ch, 1 tr into the edge of same lobe six times more, 10 ch, 2 d c into the end of the lobe, 3 d c over the bar, 2 d c into end of next lobe, 10 ch, * repeat, ending by making the last lobe like the first.

2nd Row.—Crossing behind the stem make 3 ch, 5 d c into the 1st loop, 5 ch, 5 d c into next loop, work d c into next d c's and over next loop. 2 d c into next sp, * 3 tr, 2 ch into each sp between the trs, 3 d c over the end of next two 10 ch loops, * repeat, ending the row to correspond with the beginning.

3rd Row.—Cross over behind the stem with 5 ch, and put 10 tr into 1st loop, 10 ch, 3 d c into the d c over the bar, * 10 ch, 1 d c into next sp, 4 ch, 2 tr into each sp between the trs, 4 ch, 1 d c into the sp after the trs, 10 ch, 1 d c between next 2 loops, * repeat, ending as at the beginning.

4th Row.—D c over the chs and into the trs, * 5 d c over end of next 2 loops, 7 ch, 3 tr into next sp, 4 ch,

106

3 tr into each of next 4 sp, 7 ch,
* repeat, ending as at first.

5th Row.—Work d c over the d c in
1st sp, 1 d c into the 1st and last of
the d c over the trs, 1 tr into each of
the intervening d c's, 5 ch, 1 d c
between next 2 loops, * 10 ch, 3 d c
after next trs, 6 ch, 3 d c into each of
next 3 sp, 10 ch, 1 d c between next 2
loops, * repeat, finishing with the
last lobe worked like the 1st.

Handkerchief Border and Insertion.

The edging is worked into the edge
of the handkerchief material. Use a
crochet hook having a sharp point
and Manlove's No. 60 Crochet Cotton.
Form a row of loops of 6 ch each
fastened with a d c, inserting the hook
through the material for each d c
about the 1-16th of an inch from the
edge. Put 3 loops into each corner.

2nd Row.—7 ch, 2 long tr into each
loop.

3rd Row.—5 ch, 3 d c into
each space.

4th Row.—Same as the 2nd
row.

5th Row.—Same as 3rd row.

6th Row.—2 d c in 1st sp, *
5 ch, 2 tr into next sp, 7 ch, 2
long tr into next space, 7 ch, 2
tr into next sp, 5 ch, 2 d c into
next space. * repeat.

The Insertion.

Commence with 15 ch.

1st Row.—2 d c into the 8th
ch, 6 ch, 2 d c into the 4th ch, 6
ch, 2 d c into 1st ch.

2nd Row.—* 6 ch, 2 d c into
each loop, * repeat until the
piece is long enough for a side,
break off the thread and work
on the sides of the 3 last loops,
taking care to have the strips
turned in so as to form a square.

Finish with a row of d c worked
closely over both edges.

A Crocheted Star for Pincushion Top or Inlet.

Work in Ardern's cotton, No. 40.
If coarser cotton is used, work less
ch in the loops of 18 ch.

Make foundation of 206 ch. Work
1 tr, 3 ch, 1 tr into 7th ch from needle,
5 sp (for a sp work 3 ch, miss 3 ch,
1 tr into next). Repeat 9 times from *.
Join in ring.

2nd Row.—Into the loop of 3 ch
between the 2 tr in same ch work 1
d c, 24 ch, 1 d c on tr to form loop, s c
along the 5 sp and repeat all round
from beginning.

3rd Row.—10 d c into loop of 24 ch,
6 loops of 18 ch at top of loop of 24
ch, 10 d c, 3 d c into each of the next
5 sp. Repeat all round from beginning. Break off.

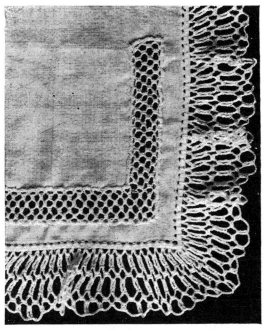

A HANDKERCHIEF BORDER
AND INSERTION.

4th Row.—1 d c into 1st loop of 18 ch, 6 ch, 1 d c into next, 6 ch, 1 d c into next, 12 ch, 1 d c into next, 6 ch, 1 d c into next, 6 ch, 1 d c into next, 18 ch, 1 d c into 2nd d c of middle sp

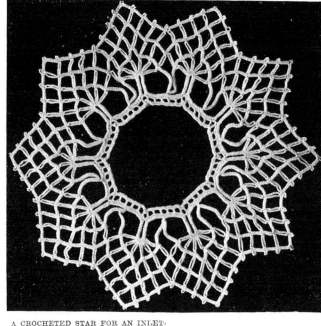

A CROCHETED STAR FOR AN INLET.

No. 40 cotton. The crochet portion is worked in two separate strips, exactly alike, one for each side; the points of the crochet "pyramids" on each side are afterwards sewn together in the middle, and a square of linen is sewn into the space between the points.

between loops of 24 ch. Repeat from beginning. Break off.

5th Row.—* 18 d c into 18 ch, loop of 18 ch over loop of 18 ch in 3rd row, 6 d c into 6 ch, loop of 18 ch, 6 d c, loop of 18 ch, 6 d c. This brings you to middle of 12 ch, here work 2 loops of 18 ch, 6 d c, loop, 6 d c, loop, 6 d c, loop, 18 d c down 18 ch. Repeat from * all round.

6th Row.—Same as 4th row, but join the 2 loops over the 18 ch together with d c.

7th Row.—Fill ch with d c and make loops over loops as in 5th row.

8th Row.—Same as 6th.

9th Row.—Same as 7th row, but instead of making loops of 18 ch make them of 5 ch and make only 1 loop in middle of the 12 ch.

Work d c all round inner side of foundation ch.

Crochet Lace with Linen Insets.

The specimen piece was worked in

1st Row.—Ch 10, 4 tr all into the 6th chain from the needle, ch 3, miss 3 ch and make 1 tr into the final ch in the foundation row.

2nd Row.—Ch 6, 1 tr into the 1st of the 4 tr in the previous row, ch 3, and then tr 4 into the little sp, ch 3 and 1 tr into same sp.

3rd Row.—Ch 6, then tr 4 into 1st little sp, ch 3, tr 4 into next sp, ch 3, tr 1 into the outer ch to form a small square space.

4th Row.—Ch 6, tr 1 into 1st of the 1st group of 4 trs in previous row, ch 3, tr 1 into 4th tr in this same group, ch 3, tr 1 into the 1st tr of the 2nd group, ch 3, then tr 4, ch 3, and tr 1 all into the final little sp.

5th Row.—Ch 6, tr 4 into 1st sp, ch 3, tr 4 into next space, ch 3, Miss a space in row below, and tr 4 into last space but one, ch 3, tr 1 into last sp.

6th Row.—Ch 6, tr 1 into 1st tr, ch 3, tr 1 into 4th tr, ch 3, tr 1 into 1st of next group of trs, ch 3, tr 1 into 4th tr. In this way make 5 holes along the row, then ch 3, and into the last sp tr 4, ch 3, and tr 1.

7th Row.—Ch 6, tr 4 into 1st sp, ch 3, tr 4 into next sp, ch 3, tr 4 into next sp but one, ch 3, tr 4 into next sp but one, ch 3, tr 1 into last sp.

8th Row.—Ch 6, tr 1 into 1st of 4 trs below, ch 3, tr 1 into 4th tr, ch 3, tr 1 into 1st tr of 2nd group, and so on, till 7 holes are made, then ch 3 and into the last sp tr 4, ch 3 and tr 1.

9th Row.—Ch 6, tr 4 into 1st sp, ch 3, tr 4 into next space, * ch 3, tr 4 into next sp but one, repeat from * twice, then ch 3, tr 1 into last sp.

10th Row.—Ch 6, tr 1 into 1st tr, ch 3, 1 tr into 4th tr, and continue to make holes all along the row till the last sp, into which tr 4, ch 3, tr 1 as in previous rows.

11th Row.—Ch 6, tr 4 into first sp, ch 3, tr 1 into the 4th tr in previous row. Then repeat from 2nd row till the piece is the length required.

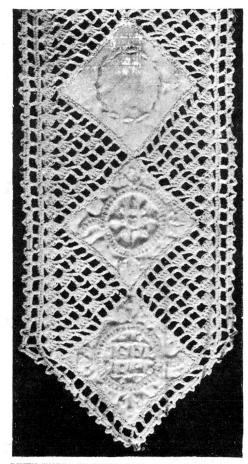

Next, strengthen the edge the linen will be sewn to, by working 3 d c into every sp up and down each side of the " pyramid," putting 6 d c into the tip of each.

Now work along the outer edge of each strip with 3 d c into every sp. Work back again along the outer edges (not the inside edges, up and down the " pyramids ") with 3 ch and 1 tr into each little sp between the groups of 3 d c just made in previous row.

To make the pointed end to the strip, with the square of linen let in —as shown in the illustration—start where the lowest " pyramid " left off, and make a ch of 60, fastening it into the corner of the lowest " pyramid" on opposite side.

Now work back, with 3 ch and 1 tr into every 3rd ch, till you have made 10 sp; then ch 6, and tr 1 into the same place for the tip, and make 10 more sp up the other side. Strengthen the inner side of this, where it will be sewn to the linen, by making 3 d c into every sp.

LINEN INSETS COMBINED WITH CROCHET
FOR TRIMMING A SUMMER BLOUSE.

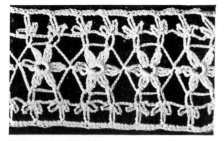

SNOWDROP INSERTION.

Finally work all the outer edge of the work (including the point) with 3 d c into every sp, and 5 ch between to form a picot edge. These picots are opened finally with the hook.

If a plain edge is required, to sew to linen, then the final edge round would be simply 3 d c into every sp, omitting the 5 ch between.

The linen insets can be embroidered or left plain, as the worker prefers.

A wider or a narrower insertion can of course be made to take any size square of linen, according to the number of rows and groups of tr

Snowdrop Insertion.

This is commenced in the centre, and Ardern's No. 40 crochet cotton will be suitable.

Make * 12 ch, form last 7 into a ring by making a single through the 5th ch, 5 ch to stand for a long tr, insert the hook through the first of the 12 ch, and make a long tr through the ring, work off the 3 loops on the needle together, and make a d c around the top of this and each of the following groups of 3 tr, 6 ch, 3 long tr into the ring 3 times, repeat from * until a long strip is formed, then turn and work the other side of the centre motif, * 6 ch, 3 long tr into the ring twice, 6 ch, 1 d c over the stitch

between this daisy and the next, repeat from * into each ring to the end.

Speedwell Insertion.

Commence with 22 ch, turn.

1 tr into the 16th ch, 3 ch, 1 tr, into the 12th ch, 3 ch, 3 tr, 4 ch, 3 tr, all into the 8th ch, 3 ch, 1 tr, into the 4th ch, 3 ch, 1 tr, into the 1st ch.

2nd Row.— * 6 ch, 1 tr into next tr, 2 tr, 4 ch, 3 tr, into next space, 3 ch, 3 tr, 4 ch, 2 tr, all into next space (after the trs), 1 tr into next tr, 3 ch, 1 tr into the next 4th ch.

3rd Row.—6 ch, 1 tr into next tr, 3 ch, into the space over the trs 3 tr, 4 ch, 3 tr, 3 ch, 1 tr into the last of next trs, 3 ch, 1 tr into the next 4th ch. * Repeat these two rows.

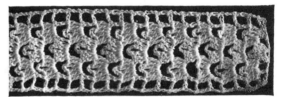

SPEEDWELL INSERTION.

Aero Edging.

Use finest feather-edge braid for this edging with Barbour's No. 80 Linen Lace Thread.

There are 4 rows of crochet at the upper portion of the braid and 5 rows in the lower portion.

Upper Rows.

1st Row.—* 1 d c into each of 1st 8 picots in the braid, 3 ch, 1 tr into each of next 5 picots, 3 ch, * repeat to the end.

2nd Row.—* 7 ch over the d c, 2 d c into first space, 2 d c, 4 ch, 2 d c into each of next 4 spaces, 2 d c into last space, * and repeat.

3rd Row.—* Over centre of the 7 ch put 6 d c, 7 ch, 2 tr into next picot,

2 ch, 2 tr into each of next 3 picots, 7 ch, * repeat.

4th Row.—2 tr, 2 ch into each space.

Lower Rows.

1st Row.—1 d c into 1st picot on the braid, * 10 ch, picot 5 of them, 5 ch, 1 d c into 2nd next picot, * repeat.

AERO EDGING.

2nd Row.—* Into the picot over the centre of the 8 d c put 3 loops of 18 ch each, 1 picot loop into each of next 5 picots, each loop made exactly like the 1st, 1 picot loop into next picot, * then repeat.

3rd Row.—* Into each of the loops of 18 ch put another of the same number with 5 ch between, 7 ch into next picot, 1 ch, 1 d c into each of next 5 picots, 7 ch, 1 d c into next loop,* repeat.

4th Row.—1 d c into 1st loop, * 7 ch, 1 d c into each of next two loops, 18 ch, 1 d c into each space between the d c's into the picots, 18 ch, 1 d c into next loop, * repeat.

5th Row.—Over 1st loop form another 18 ch loop, * 3 d c, 5 ch, 3 d c, into 1st sp, 18 ch, 3 d c, 5 ch, 3 d c,

WHEEL EDGING.

over next sp, 18 ch, 5 d c into next sp, 10 ch picot 5 of them, 5 ch, 5 d c over top of next 18 ch, 18 ch,* repeat.

Wheel Edging.

Use Ardern's No. 36 crochet cotton for this design which is suitable for a chemise top, etc.

Commence with the wheels on a 7 ch ring, 6 ch to turn, 2 tr, 3 ch, 4 times into the ring, * 6 ch to turn, 1 tr, 3 ch, 1 tr into 1st sp, turn, 6 ch, 2 tr, 3 ch 4 times into the sp, * repeat until there are 8 mitres, join in a circle and around the outer edge work a d c over each ch stitch, and connect the wheels to each other in this row, fill in the centre with 3 tr into each loop, join 1st and

last tr, and put a d c into each tr.

Commence the heading like the wheel, putting the * 2 tr, 3 ch 4 times into the ring, turn, with 6 ch * and repeat, putting the tr's into the next sp. Then finish with the d c over the ch at each side catching up the wheels in this row.

Section IX.

SOME IRISH ODDMENTS.

Bébé Irish Motif.

The finer the thread used for this make the nicer the lace will be. In No. 80 Manlove's Irish Lace Thread it is extensively used for trimming the finest kinds of babies' clothing and ladies' and children's lingerie. It is

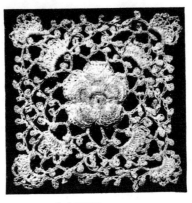

POPULAR BÉBÉ MOTIF.

also much used for trimming blouses and making collars, cuffs, etc., and is often combined with the guipure variety for that purpose.

On a two-fold padding cord form a centre ring with 15 d c, close the ring and over the padding put * 2 d c, 7 tr, 2 d c, fasten to the 3rd d c on the ring and repeat from * into every 3rd d c, this gives 5 petals in the row. Continue working round and round until there are 4 rows, each petal fastened to the d c of preceding row which fastens the petals of that row. In the 2nd row increase the number of trs in each petal by 3, and do the same for the following rows.

For the bébé filling around the rose make 12 double picot loops evenly spaced, and fasten the last to the first between the picots.

2nd Row.—* 8 ch, fasten to next loop between the picots, turn and over the 8 ch put 1 d c, 10 tr, 1 d c,

turn, 5 ch, 1 d c into every 2nd tr and over the end of the 8 ch, put a double picot loop into each of next 2, and repeat from *.

3rd Row.—A double picot loop into each loop and one into the ch before the trs, into the 2nd and 4th little loop over the trs.

4th Row.—One loop into each loop of last row and form the "group of trs" between the loop on top of preceding group and following loop. The position of the "group of trs" gives the shape to the motif, and as this is square the design can be worked into almost any shape. For "all-over" lace they are joined on every side to other motifs. Fastening the thread to a loop at the beginning of a side, between the picots, 8 ch, picot through the 3rd, 1 ch, now fasten to a corresponding loop on another motif, between the picots, 6 ch, picot 5 of them, and fasten to 2nd loop on 1st motif, then repeat the bar to opposite loops alternately.

Ivy Design for Irish Bébé Lace.

Use Barbour's Linen Lace Thread No. 40, or No. 80 for very fine work.

This design is commenced at the centre rose with three rows of

112

petals. The form of the motif is hexagonal, and when placed side by side they leave a triangular space which is filled in with a shamrock having a "Clones" knot on the centre. A single row of filling around the shamrock gives it the look of ivy-leaves and connects it with the motif at each side. A straightening line is then formed around the mitred edge and along the top. Before working the row of shamrocks at the top put a row of d c over the straightening line, then take a two-fold padding cord and work over it the shamrock edging; each petal consists of 5 d c, 5 ch, 5 d c, 5 ch, 5 d c, 5 ch, 5 d c, connected in the centre of the picots to the adjoining picots. The edge all round the mitres is formed of the same kind of shamrocks, and can very readily be copied from the illustration, and the straightening line at the top is of the usual kind.

To Make the "Clones" Knot.

This knot, so often seen in Irish crochet, requires a little practice to make it properly. Always use a

MAKING THE "CLONES" KNOT.

crochet-hook that tapers towards the point for this stitch, which is commenced on a chain the length of which depends upon the size of the knot required.

For a medium-sized knot make 7 ch, draw the loop up on the needle about an inch from the point, and placing your middle finger on it, keep it there while looping the thread over the needle above the ch, then below the ch alternately until the ch up to the 1st stitch is covered with the loops, which must be kept close together and even ; now insert the hook in the 1st ch, then thread over the needle

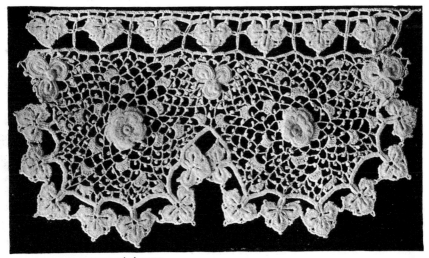

IVY DESIGN FOR IRISH BÉBÉ LACE.

Some Irish Oddments.

COIL STITCH EDGING.

and through all the loops on the needle, twisting the hook around slowly so as to let it pass smoothly through the loops, make a ch through the loop on the needle and with it pull up the knot tightly. Finish with a d c around the stem of the knot. The convex side of the knot is the right side, and this is secured with a d c into the centre on which the knot is made.

Crochet Edging with Coil Stitch Centre.

Commence on 8 ch formed into a ring, 5 ch to be concealed behind the first coil. To make the coil stitch wind the thread evenly around the needle 20 times, insert the needle in the ring and take up a loop, thread over the needle through the loop and the coil on the needle; hold the thread firmly while doing this; 1 ch into the loop on the needle, drawing up the thread at the back of the coil and having it even with it. Make 8 coils into the ring with 5 ch between them.

2nd Row.—6 d c into each sp.

3rd Row.—* 6 d c into next 6, turn, miss the 1st, 1 d c into each d c, repeat this row, missing the first in

each until there is only 1 d c in the top of the pyramid, then slipstitch to the next d c on ring and repeat from * all round.

Work a row of d c over the edges of the pyramids all round.

The motifs are joined in two points at each side while working the last row.

For the Heading.—1 d c into top of 1st pyramid on motif, * 8 ch, 1 d c into top of next pyramid, 16 ch, 1 d c into the joining of this motif and next, 8 ch, 1 single through the 8th of the 16 ch, 8 ch, 1 d into next point and repeat from * along the top.

2nd Row of Heading.—3 ch, 1 tr into every 4th stitch, finish with 4 d c into each sp.

A New Design in Bébé Irish Insertion.

Barbour's Linen Lace Thread, No. 50, is suitable for this design, except where a very fine lace is required, then No. 90 will be the best.

The half-rose centre is worked first by forming 8 ch into a ring, over half of the ring put 12 d c, turn, 5 ch, 1 d c into each 4th of 12 d c, turn, 1 d c, 10 tr, 1 d c into each loop, turn, form 3

BÉBÉ IRISH INSERTION

loops behind the last row, fastening each loop of 5 ch to the stitch between the petals on the back, turn and put 1 d c, 12 tr, 1 d c into each loop.

Turn and put a double picot loop into the 3rd and 10th tr on each petal. The double picot loop is made thus : 8 ch, catch back into the 6th to form a picot, 8 ch picot 6 of them, 2 ch, fasten with a d c.

Turn and form a 2nd row into the 1st, putting 3 picots into the 1st loop.

Turn, 8 ch, picot 6 of them, 5 ch, 1 tr into the loop between the picots, 3 ch, 1 tr into the loops before and after each picot all round.

After the tr between the last 2 picots, turn, 5 d c into each sp.

Turn, and put a 2nd row of d c into the 1st, with a 5 ch picot after every 5th d c.

This completes the motif.

Break off the thread and fasten to the d c over the tr to the left of the sp immediately above the centre leaflet, 5 ch, fasten over next tr to the right then turn and repeat from the 12 d c into the loop, fasten the filling loops to the d c's at the ends of the rows by careful spacing.

Finish with a straightening line of 5 ch, 1 tr into the centre of the d c's between the picots along each side, then a row of 6 d c into each sp.

An Irish Guipure Edging.

In this design the bébé " filling " is combined with a " guipure " edge. Form a four-fold padding cord and with No. 60 Irish lace thread make a centre ring of the double padding into which put 30 d c. Close the ring. 10 d c over the cord into first 10 on the ring, 7 d c over the cord alone. * 20 tr, 2 d c, 1 d c over the cord and through the 3rd d c before the trs taking in the cord there also ; this forms the trs into a petal, 2 d c and repeat from * twice more. The cord is carried down beside the stem and d c worked over it and the cord in the other side together. 10 d c over the cord into next 10 on the ring, * 20 d c over cord alone, turn this back and fasten to the centre tr on the 1st petal of the shamrock with a d c, * repeat and fasten to each leaflet and to the first d c in the second row.

D c over the cord into remaining stitches on ring, then into first 20 as far as the top of the 1st petal on the shamrock, over padding alone 1 d c,

AN IRISH GUIPURE EDGING

Some Irish Oddments.

12 tr, 3 d c, turn, miss the 3 d c, 1 d c into 1st tr, 1 tr into each tr, 1 d c, 2 d c into next 2 on next 20 d c, turn and repeat the leaflet, putting the 1st 7 tr in the last trs of 1st row ; form 9 leaflets in this way, having the last exactly opposite the 1st, complete the d c into last 20 and fasten off the padding on the back, then cut away the superfluous thread. With No. 80 Irish lace thread work the 3 rows of bébé filling around the top portion, putting a single picot in each loop and a group of trs in place of the 3rd loop at each side from the leaflets.

To connect the motifs fasten the thread to the loop above the group of trs, make 4 ch and join to the end tr in another motif, then a picot bar, fasten to the last tr in 1st motif, a plain bar to 1st tr in 2nd motif, a picot bar to 1st tr in 1st motif, a plain bar into next loop, then so on to the leaflet. Make 4 ch and fasten to the top of leaflet to the right, turn and over this bar put 4 d c, 5 ch, 4 d c. Fasten off neatly on the back.

With the coarser thread make the straightening lines at the top of the edging, 4 ch, 1 tr into each loop before the picot and into the top of each "group" and connecting loop.

Over the ch stitches work a row of d c closely.

Make a second row of 4 ch, 1 tr into the d c over the trs of 1st row and finish with a row of close d c over the chain stitches.

Crochet Appliqué on Net.

Crochet appliqué on net is a favourite mode for blouse trimming and yokes, as well as for underskirts, camisole tops, etc., the design shown here being suitable for insetting, the material being cut to fit the lace.

The edges are first worked over with buttonhole stitch ; the lace is then top-sewn neatly to the stitching on the back.

Cut the net in the shape shown in the illustration. With a moderately coarse mercerised cotton work a row of d c into the meshes at the upper edge, putting the hook through the second row of meshes from the edge. At the lower side put 2 d c into each mesh, work * 10 d c, 8 ch, turn to the right and fasten to the 5th d c, turn into the loop, 3 d c, 6 ch, 3 d c, 6 ch, 3 d c, 6 ch, 3 d c, repeat from * to the end.

For the motif, make a ring of 9 ch, into which put 12 d c, 1 d c into 1st d c, * 12 ch, turn, 1 d c into 11th ch, 1 tr into each ch except the 1st, into which put 1 d c, 1 d c into 1st d c. on ring (that is, into the same stitch as the last), 1 d c into next, then repeat from * seven times more.

Sew the motif to the net on the centre of an oval, turning the back of the work towards you and using the same kind of thread for the purpose.

Silver and Gold Thread Crochet.

Crochet in silver and gold threads is suitable for adorning evening dresses. It is made up into blouses, yokes, etc., and insertions for trimming net blouses which are embroidered with the silver thread. Bags can also be made of it, either for evening use or for mounting on velvet for wearing with the costume.

Use a coarse crochet needle as the

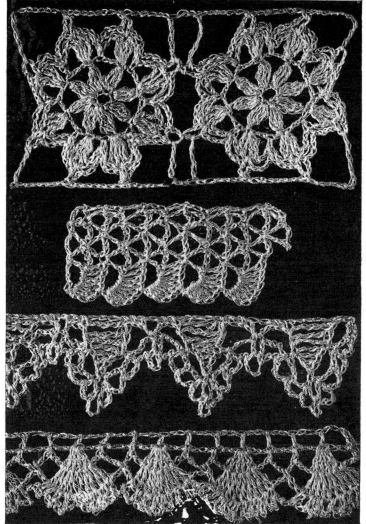

DESIGNS IN SILVER AND GOLD THREAD CROCHET.

work must be done rather loosely but evenly.

Design I.

The Design at the top shows a pretty motif which is very easily made into "all-over" lace for blouses, and into insertion for trimmings.

Commence on 8 ch joined into a ring, into each ch put a group of 3 long tr, retaining the last loop in each until finishing the third, when you work off all the loops on the needle together, 3 ch between the groups.

2nd Row.—Slip-stitch to the second ch, * 2 ch, 1 tr 2 long tr 1 tr all into the stitch over next group of trs, 2 ch 1 d c into next second ch, and repeat from *.

3rd Row.—* 4 ch 1 d c into the space between the long trs, 5 ch 1 d c into same space, 4 ch 1 d c into next d c, * repeat.

117

Silver and Gold Thread Crochet.

The motifs are joined in two picots while making, to the corresponding picots on next motif.

For insertion connect the motifs in a straight line, then for the straightening, * 6 ch 1 d c into each of the two picots on the top, 6 ch 1 long tr into the first picot in the joining, 2 ch 1 long tr into the second picot in the joining, * repeat along both sides.

Design II.

This is a pretty edging for collars, sleeves, fronts, etc.; 14 ch, turn, 1 tr into the ninth ch, 3 ch 1 tr into the same ch, 1 tr into the sixth ch, 3 ch 1 tr into the same ch, 5 ch 1 d c into the first ch, turn, * 1 d c 7 tr over the 5 ch, 1 tr into the top of next tr, 3 ch 1 tr into same stitch as last, 1 tr over next tr, 3 ch 1 tr into same stitch as last, 1 tr into next ch, turn.

3 ch 1 tr into last tr, 1 tr over next trs, 3 ch 1 tr into same stitch as last, 1 tr into next tr, 3 ch 1 tr into same stitch as last, 5 ch 1 d c into next fifth tr, repeat from *.

Design III.

This is a pretty vandyke edging made on a length of chain stitches.

1st Row.—* 3 d c into next 3 ch, 5 ch, 3 d c into next 3 ch, 7 ch, 1 d c into the 5th ch, 1 tr into the 4th, 1 long tr into the 3rd, 1 triple tr into the 2nd, and 1st ch, and into the side of the d c, lay last long tr along the chs and fasten with a d c, then repeat from *.

2nd Row.—Fasten the thread to the top of the 1st picot, * 5 ch, 1 d c into the picot, 5 ch, 1 d c into the 3rd tr up the side, into the point twice and into the opposite side of the 3rd tr, and into next picot, then repeat from *.

3rd Row.—* 5 ch picot into the 1st picot, 2 ch, 1 d c into next d c, 5 ch, 1 d c into next 3rd ch, 5 ch, 1 d c into next d c, 5 ch, 1 d c into the picot twice, 5 ch, 1 d c into next d c, 5 ch, 1 d c into next, 3 ch, 5 ch, 1 d c into d c, 2 ch, 1 d c into next picot, into which repeat from *.

Design IV.

This is also commenced on a row of ch.

1st Row.—2 ch, 1 tr into every 3rd ch.

2nd Row.— 1 d c over 1st tr, * 2 ch, 5 tr into next tr, 2 ch, 1 d c into next tr, 5 ch, 1 d c into next tr, * repeat.

3rd Row.—* d c into centre of 5 ch, 2 ch, 2 tr into each tr, 2 ch, * repeat.

4th Row.—3 ch, 1 d c into every tr and between the groups.